A typical Canary bal

DECIMOPRIMERA EDICION

© by EDITORIAL EVEREST, S. A.
Carretera León-La Coruña, km 5 - LEON (Spain)
All rights reserved
ISBN: 84-241-4606-9
Legal deposit: 130-1989
The total or partial reproduction
of this book is forbidden
Printed in Spain

EDITORIAL EVERGRAFICAS, S. A.
Carretera León-La Coruña, km 5
LEON (Spain)

TENERIFE
LA PALMA
GOMERA
HIERRO

Texts: Enrique García Ramos

Photographs: J. Ciganovic
Juan M. Ruiz

AL MERITO TURISTICO
MINISTERIO DE INFORMACION Y TURISMO — ESPAÑA

Editorial Everest, S. A.

MADRID • LEON • BARCELONA • SEVILLA • GRANADA
VALENCIA • ZARAGOZA • BILBAO • LAS PALMAS DE GRAN
CANARIA • LA CORUÑA – MEXICO • BUENOS AIRES

I

BETWEEN AFRICA AND EUROPE

Some sixty miles from the coast of Africa, separated from it by a wide strip of Atlantic waters, there is an archipelago which is at the same time an advance post of Europe and a bridge with the lands of America. Seven islands of different areas, which go from rather more than two thousand square kilometres to about three hundred, compose the Canaries, which are accompanied by an escort of islets of various shapes and sizes. Barely two hours by plane and less than two days by ship separate them from Madrid and the ports in the south of the Iberian Peninsula respectively, and a flight from the most distant of European capitals to any of the great transatlantic airports they possess will not take more than six hours.

The miles of sea that, separate the islands from the black continent soften the harshness of the climate of the Sahara, and what on the mainland is rigour and drought becomes mild temperatures, marine freshness and the song of water in the islands. In special contrast, the not too distant sands and dry stones of the desert are transformed into rich valleys full of vegetation, densely wooded mountains and intensely cultivated plains. However, not everything in the Canaries is subtropical, nor does the green of plants entirely dominate the surface of the islands, for they alternate with bare, aggressive peaks, very ancient torrent beds with steep banks which forgot the caress of water millenia ago, and other regions where powerful geological forces are grandly displayed.

The Canary Islands seem to concentrate in little more than seven thousand square kilometres the essence of the entire planet, and their special mountain system with varied heights provides aspects as different from one another as the Canadian forests and the unhospitable deserts of the interior of Australia. It is in this that the charm of the archipelago chiefly resides.

The Canary Islands have been known since remote times. Many say

The Canary Islands in the «Catalan Atlas of 1375», probably the work of Abraham and Jafudá Crosques.

that they gave rise to the beautiful myth of the Hesperides, and between legend and reality, between stories of untruthful mariners of the ancient world who dared to pass the pillars of Hercules and some relatively accurate descriptions by scholars, the Middle Ages were ending with the archipelago converted into a remote and even dangerous place, whose situation was hardly known. It was in 1130 that the veil of mystery began to be torn thanks to an expedition sent out by Alfonso IV of Aragon. Many years passed, however, before interest was resumed, when in the early 15th century the Norman adventurer Jean de Bethancourt

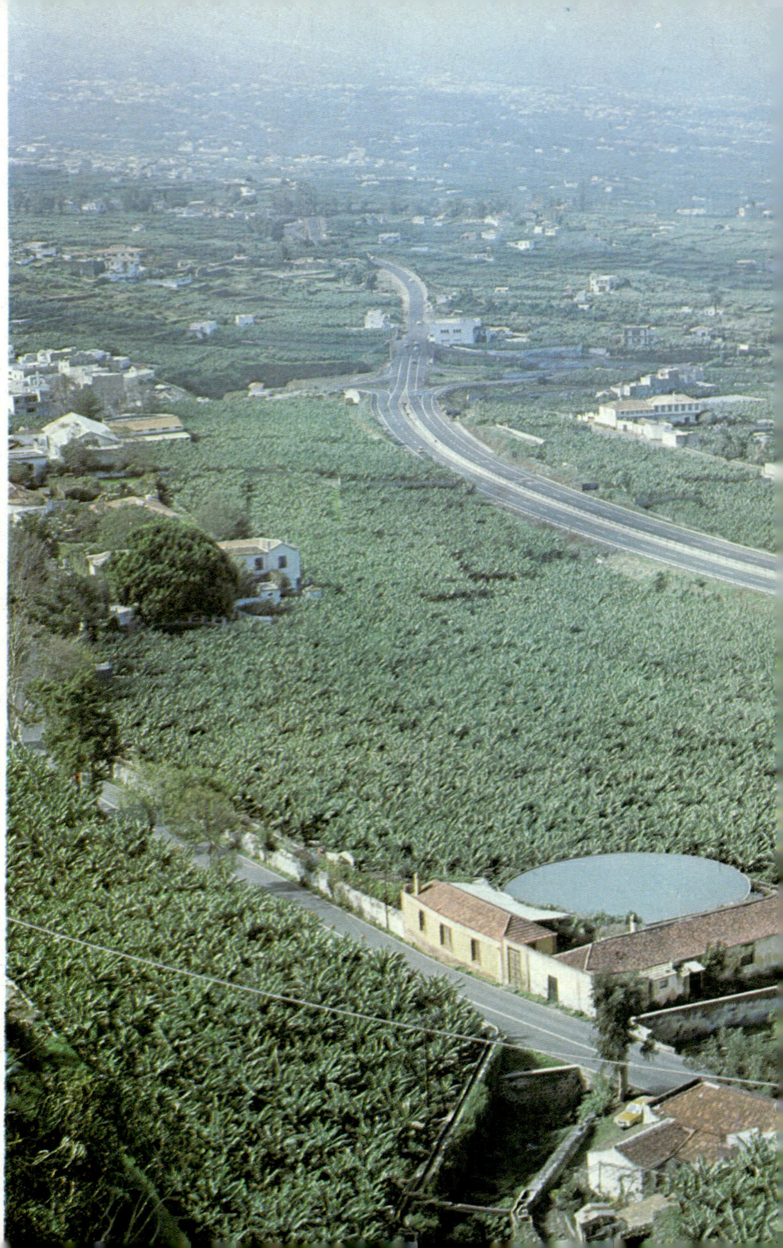

The scenery of Tenerife is seen at its best in the Valley of La Orotava.

took possession of the more easterly islands. His nephew Maciott, who replaced him in the sort of viceroyship which had been implanted, finding himself in difficulties of a military end economic nature, ceded them to the kingdom of Portugal until Spain, a little later, recovered the sovereignty which the Castilian monarchs had acquired, and it was then, after the conquest of the remaining islands, that the Canaries were opened to the civilised world of the epoch and integrated, after not a few vicissitudes, into the European context.

Rather more than 1,200,000 people inhabit the seven principal islands, at present divided into two provinces after having formed only one until 1927, with its capital in Santa Cruz de Tenerife. Now the two provinces are Santa Cruz de Tenerife, with its capital in the island of Tenerife, which also includes those of La Palma, La Gomera and El Hierro, and Las Palmas, with its capital of the same name, in the island of Gran Canaria, which forms a province with those of Fuerteventura and Lanzarote.

The Canary climate is very varied, cooler in the western islands because of the Atlantic winds and a little hotter in the eastern zone, where the trade-winds meet with another type of opposition and the nearby Sahara has an influence. However, the great regulator of the marine mass concedes the benefit of mildness and the existence of harsh conditions can hardly be indicated.

Despite their nickname of the Fortunate Islands, the Canaries did not always offer an easy life to their inhabitants who, although they enjoyed the pleasant climate, had to harden themselves for centuries in the struggle against Berber invaders in search of booty and impressive fleets of European powers that wanted to take over the magnificent enclave that the archipelago formed with regard to communications with America. Between farmer and warrior, between fisherman and discoverer, the islander was forging his special way of being, which in spite of his apparent indolence has enabled him to perform a task that has already lasted a century and a half, and is no more or less than to «manufacture» the earth in which he has achieved the miracle of raising complicated crops, of selecting vegetable species, of digging into the bowels of the earth in search of water with which to irrigate the zones open to cultivation, and in short to create riches out of nothing. It has been, and still is, a gigantic labour to transport earth from dozens of kilometres away in order to cover the harsh, stony soil of the old volcanic zones by constructing enormous «flower-pots» and fashioning terraces on the mountain slopes which have enabled them to reach our days with magnificent agricultural exploitations.

Cane plantations and the subsequent preparation of sugar; rich vineyards, which have made the name of Tenerife sound all over Europe

Landscape at Arguayo, with the typical terraces for cultivation.

View of the Valley of Arriba, in the municipality of Santiago del Teide.

A typical country house at Garachico, surrounded by banana trees.

The dragon tree at the seminary of La Laguna is one of the most famous in Tenerife.

The banana is the most important crop in the Canaries.

thanks to the famous malmsey which Shakespeare praised through the mouth of Falstaff; cochineal, a colouring matter from animal sources, much in demand in the textile industry until the discovery of aniline dyes, tobacco, etc., until we reach the banana and tomato, present lords of the islands' agriculture and exports. This, in broad lines, between fighting and working, has been the progress of the Canaries during centuries of History.

II

TENERIFE, A CONTINENT IN MINIATURE

Tenerife, the biggest island in the Canaries, has an area of about 2.000 square kilometres; it was the centre and capital of the archipelago until a few decades ago and today still keeps the directing of certain political and administrative aspects. In Tenerife we find the peak of Teide, an old volcano 3,718 metres above sea level which is the highest point in Spanish territory. With its summit nearly always covered with snow it dominates the region, and its imposing coneshaped mass is the first thing sailors see as they approach the islands.

The city of Santa Cruz de Tenerife looks over a sheltered bay on the north-east coast; it is the capital of the province, half surrounded by fascinating mountains, a sample of what the island is as it rises in a stony mass that does not look as if it will provide any shelter as we draw near it, for except for certain zones the rise is steep, almost sheer, as it gains height and originates a really striking variety of climates. Once we have set foot on the island our first impression makes way for another, as we see to our surprise how different it is from what it appeared. Thanks to the diversity of altitudes, in an hour we can pass from the enlivening warmth of a beach to the cold of a high mountain. The bather sunning himself in the north of the island often does so while he admires broad snowy slopes little more than a dozen kilometres away. As one moves further inland, the tropical crops of the coast change into vegetation of the temperate zone, which are later transformed into samples of the flora and woods of northern Europe. You can go water-skiing in the morning and skate on ice after lunch, spend some hours in a bathingdress and then change into sturdy mountain boots and wool-lined jackets so as not to feel cold on a trip to other zones.

These characteristics have granted the island of Tenerife a title which many travellers have applied to it, that of a little continent, with its

View of Santa Cruz de Tenerife, from the harbour.

The Bailadero (Dance Place) in the mountainous peninsula of Anaga, in the North of the island.

The Teide, from Las Mercedes mountain, in the mountainous massif of Anaga.

The beautiful, peaceful Médano beach.

Puerto de la Cruz is the tourist capital of Tenerife.

tremendous variety of scenery and even of the architecture of its towns and villages.

Tenerife ranks as the first port in Spain with regard to the movement and tonnage of ships, and its ample harbours are nearly always occupied by all kinds of vessels, from the supertanker bringing crude for the refinery or the finished product for Europe to the luxury liner with thousands of passengers on board, vessels of the steamship lines, cargo ships and deep-water fishing craft. The oil refinery installed near Santa Cruz in 1930 has meant a great impulse for the port, though since long before it has been frequented by ships of all nationalities on the routes to America and South Africa.

Of volcanic construction, like its sisters, the island of Tenerife is an enormous stony mass of basalt and granite, of solidified lava which in the course of thousand and thousans of years has gradually beeneroded by the elements until it has filled with vegetation. The natural process, spectacular in itself, has been increased by the colossal labour of the islanders, who have made gardens, installed terraces on the steep mountain slopes of their land until they have transformed extensive zones into real flower gardens.

Those who arrive in Tenerife for the first time often fall into the error of identifying its inhabitants with the original people of the island, the Guanches. Of that race, notable for its nobility, physical strength and brave spirit of independence, only the memory remains, plus a very few drops of blood among a small minority. The shock between two worlds as different as the Guanche pastoral society, living in the polished stone age, and that of the Spanish conquerors ended, as usually happens, in the extinction of the conquered, due more to the Guanches' own wish than to the harshness of their masters. Beautifully worked stones, strangely mummified bodies, objects of bone and clay remind us, in museums, of a people of white race and mysterious origin that was the victim of the rush of civilisation. Not all the aboriginese of the Canaries were Guanches, for these were only the ones who inhabited Tenerife and were quite different in features and aspect from their nearby neighbours in the other islands, with whom they had no communication as they hardly knew the art of navigation. However, names like Tinerfe, Beneharo, Ruyman and Tinguaro and surnames like Bencomo and Tahoro are a heritage or memory of the powerful men with light skin and sometimes light blue eyes, dressed in sheep or goat skins, who with their beautiful women trod the paths of the then unknown island.

The present Tinerfeños (people of Tenerife) descend from the Spanish conquerors who little by little settled in the island, and many of them have grandparents, and even parents, born in the most varied corners

Reconstitution of a «guanche» tomb in the Archeological Museum of Santa Cruz de Tenerife.

One of the rooms in the important Archeological Museum of Santa Cruz.

Old cannons at Paso Alto Castle, in the port of Santa Cruz de Tenerife.

of the Peninsula, not forgetting those who have Irish, Flemish or Germanic ancestors who, driven by the political and religious struggles which devastated Europe in other times or because of commercial or seafaring activities, established themselves in the island.

Forthcoming in joys and reserved in sorrows, the Tinerfeños have come to form a variegated and cosmopolitan nucleus due to the emigration currents and their ever continued contacts with many countries. Cuba and Venezuela, until a short time ago, Argentina and Uruguay, where they arrived to found cities and create nuclei like Montevideo, and even the United States, know of the Tinerfeños who, in search of wider horizons, crossed the seas to work for the expansion of new countries. On the other side, commercial relations with Great Britain, Germany, France and Scandinavia have been very intense since the 19th century; the incessant contact with intercontinental travellers who put in at the port, and the long stays for rest and recreation of thousands of foreigners, have given the Tinerfeños a special way of understanding things and an uncommon sense of looking at things on the large scale.

III

SANTA CRUZ

Bordered by craggy mountains and gazing over the sea, the capital of the island and the province is a mixture of the old colonial style which adopted unusual forms, and of architectural modernism. Typical old streets, broad tree-lined avenues, well planned gardens and very modern commercial arteries go to make up Santa Cruz, which from its original nucleus has been spreading and adapting itself until it has become a city of our time. The traveller who arrives in the splendid port by sea will first be surprised by squares and gardens in which artistic and historical monuments relate something of the history of the city, and later will find himself in crowded, bustling streets, lit up at night by the many-coloured brightness of advertisements and the shop-windows of international trade in which, together with the most modern and complicated electronic apparatus, he can see silks from India, porcelain from China and most beautiful works of art in jade and ivory. Tenerife's strategic situation in the great world routes has made this commerce flourish as it sells to travellers passing through and tourists spending a holiday here, besides the inhabitants of the island themselves. Like a carelessly hung tapestry, the districts of the upper zone give their note of colour, while at a distance, towards

Urban corner of Santa Cruz of Tenerife in the neuralgic centre of the city.

Anaga Avenue, from the Plaza de España.

Urban perspective of the Marina street.

one of the ends of the city, the fires from the ventilation shafts of the great oil refinery and the tall chimneys of the industrial zone can be seen.

The capital of the province contains more than 180,000 inhabitants in its urban nucleus, but the fact that it is the nerve centre of the island and the constant visit of tourists means that it has a considerably greater floating population.

Santa Cruz de Tenerife is the seat of the Captain General of the Archipelago and of the African provinces of Sahara. This military official is housed in a fine edifice built at the end of last century which faces a beautiful square called after General Weyler, to whom the construction of the Captain's palace was due. This square occupies what was, until a few years ago, the geographical centre of the island; from it there lead the broad Rambla de Pulido, going to the upper and modern town, mainly a residential zone, and an artery which in one direction crosses a high bridge on its way to the industrial zone, and in the other comes to the Avenida de Anaga which skirts the harbour after passing through the Municipal Park. This is a well kept garden of about six hectares, the real lung of the city, in the middle of which is a monument erected in honour of an illustrious Tinerfeño, while the side walks, lakes, fountains and arcades are decorated with sculptures dedicated to famous people and the muses.

The fountain in the centre of the Plaza de Weyler is worth a mention, the work of Italian craftsmen of last century.

Nearby is the Palace of the Municipal Council of the Island, an imposing building crowned by a high tower in which, besides numerous administrative services of this body, which is equivalent to a provincial deputation, there is an interesting Island Museum with many examples of the culture and customs of the aborigenes.

In what we might call the old town is the ancient church of Our Lady of the Conception, in which is kept the cross that the conqueror and first governor of the island, Fernández de Lugo, brought with him, and other historical and religious relics of great value. Santa Cruz has a well stocked Municipal Library and a select picture gallery. Among its educational centres are the Official School of Navigation and Machinery, the School of Commerce and the Institute of Secondary Education, in two buildings situated in different parts of the city that deal with both masculine and feminine education. Other cultural and recreational centres are the Fine Arts Club, a real source of encouragement for beautiful manifestations of the spirit; the Provincial Music Conservatory, which has produced most of the members of the Tenerife Symphony Orchestra and distinguished artists; the Principal Club, which devotes special attention to musical events of international prestige and to lectures

Place of España corner and Castillo street.

by world-famous figures, attended by all the society of the island; the Yacht Club, with its sporting and social aspects; the Twelfth of January Friendship Club, a place of recreation for the citizens; the Mercantile Club, in a beautiful building, and other bodies and societies with a high reputation.

Santa Cruz de Tenerife has a history full of heroism which justifies its titles of Very Loyal, Noble and Unconquered and Charitable. From its early days, when it was hardly more than a group of fishermen's huts, merchant's warehouses and an inn for sailors, it knew the thunder of cannon and the din of battle. Its old forts made history by repelling the successive attempts at conquest by the fleets of Jennings and Blake, and a century and a half later that of Horatio Nelson; the great British sailor knew the bitter taste of defeat for the first time when faced by the valour of the Tinerfeños, after losing his right arm, when he had to sign the surrender of his troops and ships to an enemy that, almost without means, excelled itself by beating the most illustrious seaman of his times. The flags and standards taken from the conquered Englishman are a valued treasure kept in the old fort of Paso Alto, now converted into a museum of the feat; in it, overlooking the sea, is the bronze cannon called «Tiger», whose broadside «killed the daring Bowen; took an arm off Nelson, and with one ball killed twenty-two of the defeated English», as a poet of the day described the episode.

Later, Tenerife and its men went on making history during the course of the 19th century and Santa Cruz was always present in all important events that agitated the nation, down to our own times.

Let us return to the present day, leaving on one side what happened in other times, to add that Santa Cruz, without forgetting its past, is struggling in the present and looking towards the future and hoping to excel itself, while it lives, works and amuses itself intensely. Its famous Winter Fiestas, in the Carnivals, are a whole course of popular gaiety and civic conduct; of knowing how to have a good time and how to respect others. Large groups of musicians, choirs, troupes of dancers, comic groups, carriages, fancy dress and good taste unite in this explosive display of amusement which brings thousands of visitors to the island.

The theatre is a favourite entertainment, and luxurious premises for shows, night clubs, discothèques and other attractions complete the picture of festive Santa Cruz; if it is good to work, it is also good to amuse ourselves when our duties have been completed. A bullring and a large football stadium, besides smaller sports grounds, cater for a great many tastes.

The capital communicates with the rest of the island by two wide roads which start from the same point in the outskirts of the city

Santa Cruz de Tenerife. Square and the Candelaria monument. ▶

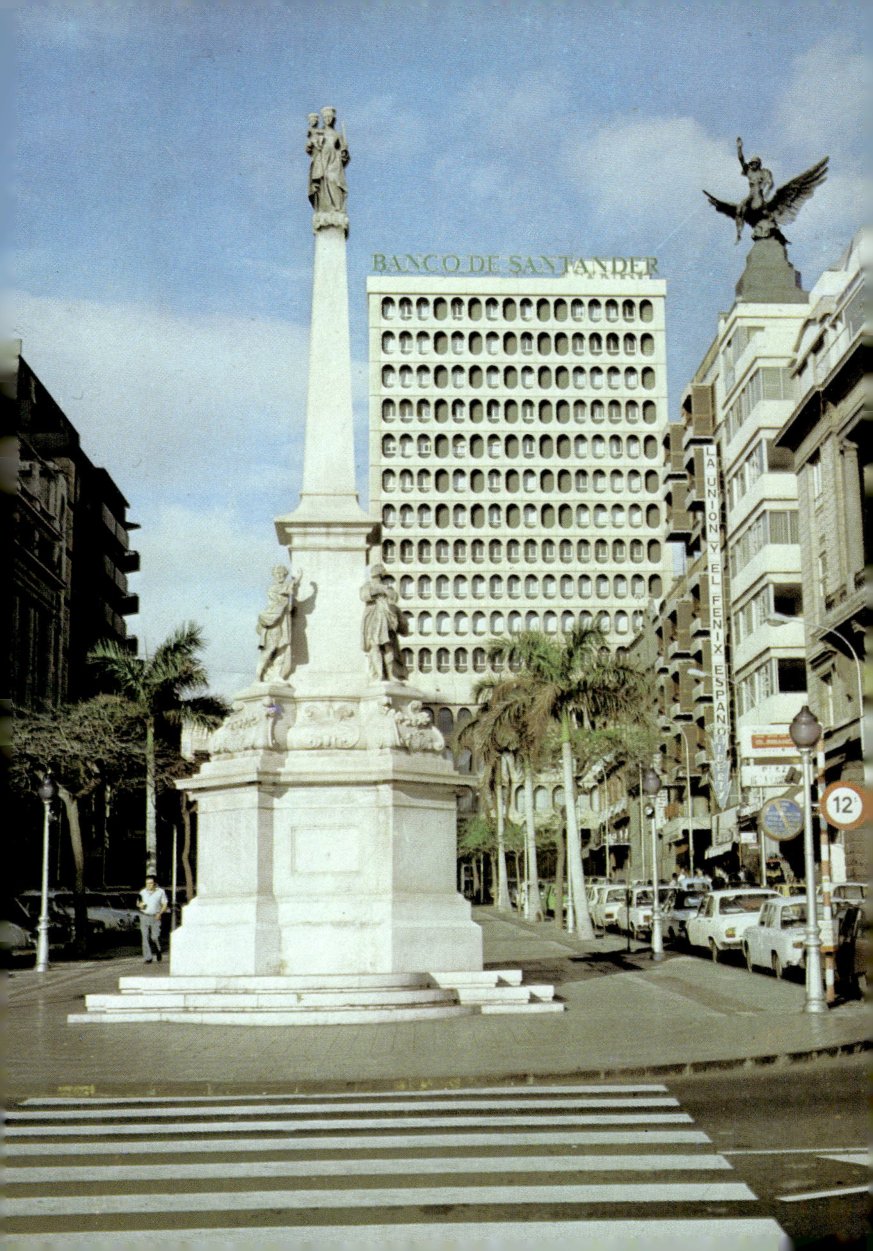
BANCO DE SANTANDER
LA UNION Y EL FENIX ESPAÑOL
12t

Santa Cruz de Tenerife. St. Francis' Church.

Santa Cruz de Tenerife. The beautiful gardens of the Plaza de la Paz.

and then branch off, one to the North and the other to the South. There is also an old road, almost parallel to the motorway, which goes to La Laguna and the northern region, and another road to San Andrés and Igueste de San Andrés with a branch to Taganana, all these being fishing and farming villages. San Andrés, a few minutes from Santa Cruz by the Coast Road, is beginning to «take off» touristically as beside it is the great beach of «Las Teresitas» with more than a kilometre and a half of golden sand, which has recently been reconditioned for bathers and boating by means of the installation of a semi-submerged mole running along all its length, which eliminates any possible dangerous currents.

IV

LA LAGUNA, ON THE ROAD TO THE NORTH

Using the motorways mentioned in the previous chapter, the journey to other points in the island is confortable and rapid. We shall now refer to one of the zones most frequentod by visitors, the North, though we have already mentioned what may be seen in the course of the trip. The temperature is normally pleasant and the sun shines, although from time to time, especially in the winter months, it may rain as is meet and right, as the liturgy says. Following the Motorway to the North we first skirt the south-east side of Santa Cruz; after a wide curve with a gentle gradient we enter a long straight stretch, always climbing, until we reach La Laguna, nine kilometres from the capital. This is the oldest city in the island of Tenerife, for it was the first to be founded by the conqueror and first governor, Alonso Fernández de Lugo as a residence for himself and his captains. Its severe rectilinear plan therefore recalls the Castilian style rather, and La Laguna, 450 metres above sea level, in the centre of a moist, fertile valley, has a severe and almost monastic aspect. Silence and peace are its distinctive notes and its long streets are lined with old buildings and ancient mansions with coast-of-arms over their doors, showing the rank of those who raised them. The peculiar Canary balconies, made of indestructible candlewood, hang over the streets and their thick grilles prevent the curious from looking inside, where an elderly and dusty lady may sometimes be discerned, employing her leisure with rich and complicated embroidering.

It is an episcopal seat, and the bishop's palace has a stone façade

Detail of the façade of La Laguna Cathedral.

Interior of La Laguna Cathedral.

The interesting font in the Church of the Conception, in La Laguna.

and artistic grilles protecting its windows and balconies. The Cathedral, built to replace the old church of Los Remedios at the beginning of this century, has slender lines and is neoclassical in style. Another church of special interest if that of Our Lady of the Conception, an ancient parish church of large dimensions, declared a national monument and crowned by a daring, lofty bell-tower of dry stone. The carpenters' work produced a choir of exceptional quality, and the pulpit, carved from noble woods, is a jewel of baroque art. Two old and enormous enclosed convents, of the Poor Clares and the nuns of St. Catharine, stand out with their great, severe masses. La Laguna is severe and attractive at the same time. Old palaces, such as that of the Marquises of Nava in dark stone of the country, contribute to this. The Sanctuary of Christ, by which is a convent of Franciscan nuns, contains one of the most beautiful sculpures of the Crucified, late Gothic in style, due to a great but unknown Italian artist; this image is the centre of the islanders' religious devotion.

There is another side to La Laguna, for its nearly sixty thousand inhabitants do not live only as memories of a great past. La Laguna is the university centre of the archipelago; its University of St. Ferdinand is spacious and modern, with its escort of residential colleges and auxiliary centres. Its faculties are Law, Philosophy and Letters, Chemical Sciences, Biology and Medicine, to which must be added the first Section of Journalism to be founded in Spain when this profession was included amongst the higher studies. Other teaching centres in the city are the technical schools of Agricultural Engineers and Construction, the Teaer'chers' School and the Institute of Secondary Education. Cultural societies such as the Athenaeum, and of types that vary from the artistic one of the Orfeón La Paz to the recreational one of the Casino, maintain a very active life.

The plain of La Laguna is a marvel of verdure. It is very extensive, and bordered by the mountain ranges that only leave a passage to the south and the north-west and a narrow access to the east; it is prolonged in the cool plains of Los Rodeos, towards which the motorway continues. Barely three kilometres from the city is the Tenerife airport, which took its name from the district where it was established; in the last decade it received a great impulse when it was enlarged, which enables it to deal with intense traffic. Planes from all countries land and take off there. The giants of the air mingle with the rapid little planes that communicate regularly with the other islands; in spite of the size of the existing installations, they will soon be used as auxiliary ones, for another great transoceanic airport is being prepared in the south of the island. There is an immensely active aeroclub.

The old wheat-growing lands of Los Rodeos are changing a little.

La Laguna. St. Catharine's Convent. In the background, the palace of the Marquises of Villanueva del Prado.

SAN FRANCISCO
REAL SANTUARIO
DEL
SANTISIMO CRISTO
DE
LA LAGUNA

St. Francis' Monastery. Exterior and altar of the Most Holy Christ of La Laguna.

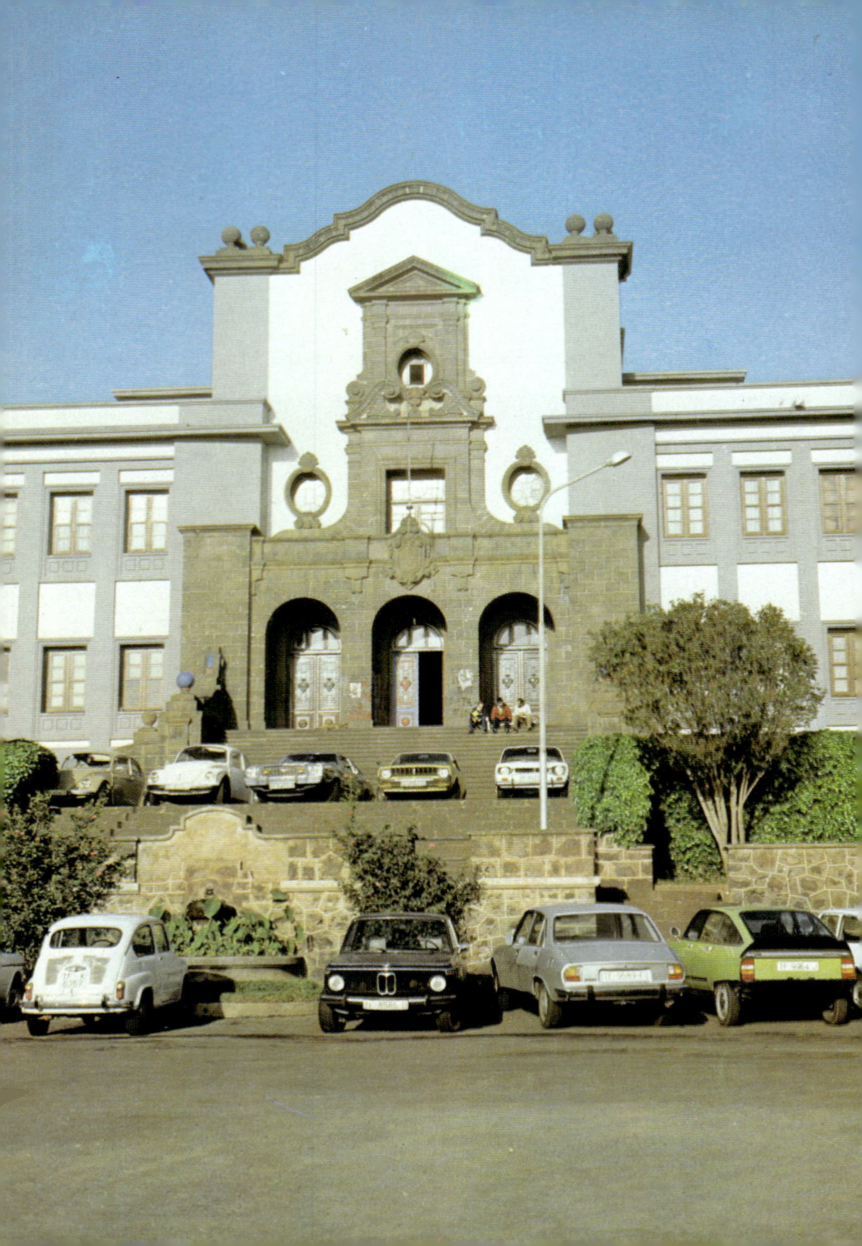

La Laguna. Monument to Father Anchieta, the evangelizer of Brazil.

◀ Central biulding of La Laguna University.

Many houses and villas are occupying zones in which formerly the wheat swayeod in the breeze, but the change has not been so profound as to destroy the peculiar bucolic aspect of the region.

To the north-west, cutting short the gently climbing plain, is the massif in the background of which we can make out the majestic Teide, which stands out from afar on clear days. Towards Tacoronte, which recently received the title of city, the traveller continues to the north. Tacoronte is a farming town with a famous harsh red wine. It has a sanctuary in which a baroque carved image of Christ is venerated, which reminds one of the Crucified of The Victories in Seville. The motorway goes on and soon runs through El Sauzal, divided into two districts, the upper and the coastal. The former has vineyards capable of producing high proof wine, while the latter, beside the sea, where banana plantations now begin, has its green tones often dotted with the bright light colours of villas and houses looking over the waters of both the sea and their own swimming pools and those of the neighbouring tourist centres. La Matanza, a farming place which maintains the tradition of red wine and in the seasons of the vintage and pressing smells of must and freshly cut grass, hangs over the original road and seems to want to forget, in silence and almost asleep, the last great warlike exploit of the aborigines when they almost completely destroyed the troops of the conqueror Fernández de Lugo, thus giving the place and the zone their name (Matanza means Slaughter). A few kilometres away is La Victoria, which also has warlike memories, for it was here that Fernández de Lugo obtained complete revenge for the defeat he had suffered a year before and broke the resistance of the Guanches. Further on is Santa Ursula, now right in the dominion of the banana tree, until we come to the splendid valley of La Orotava.

V

THE VALLEY OF LA OROTAVA

They say that the great naturalist Alexander Humboldt, when he visited Tenerife in the late 18th century, knelt on the ground and wept with emotion while he gave thanks to the Almighty for having let him contemplate the beauty of the Valley of La Orotava, which appears, almost suddenly, before the visitor when he rounds one of the pieces of high ground that had hidden it. The fact is that this anecdote, which all Tinerfeños know and are proud of, must be true,

A typical Canary patio in Tacoronte.

Tacoronte. Façade of the church.

The much venerated Christ of the Sorrows (c. 18) of Tacoronte.

A street in El Sauzal, dominated by its church tower. ▶

View of El Sauzal; the Teide in the background.

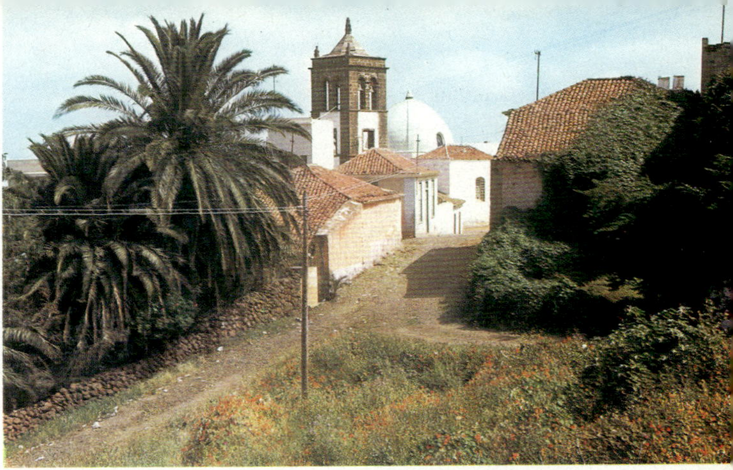

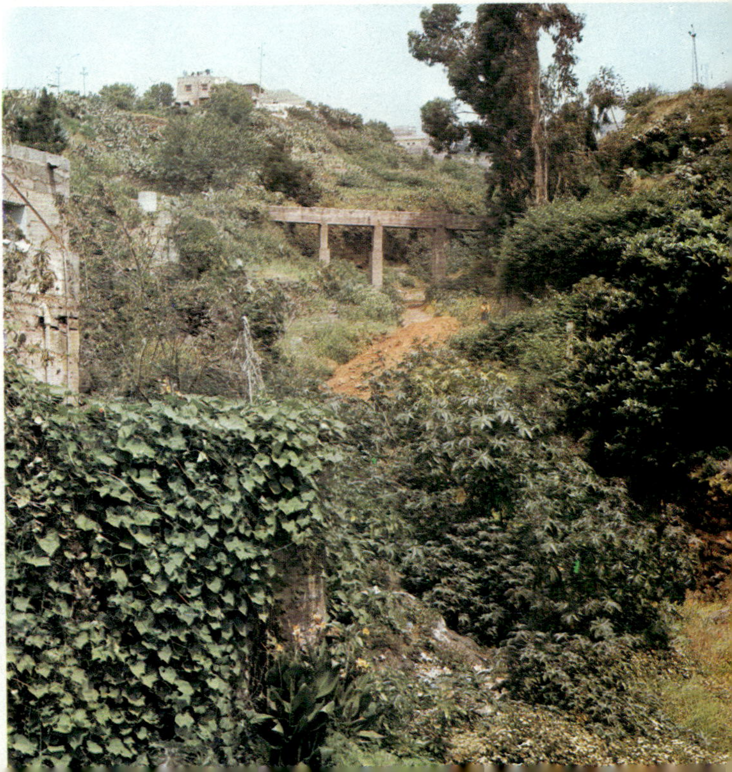

View of the beautiful town of La Orotava.

The gorge of San Antonio in the Victoria de Acentejo.

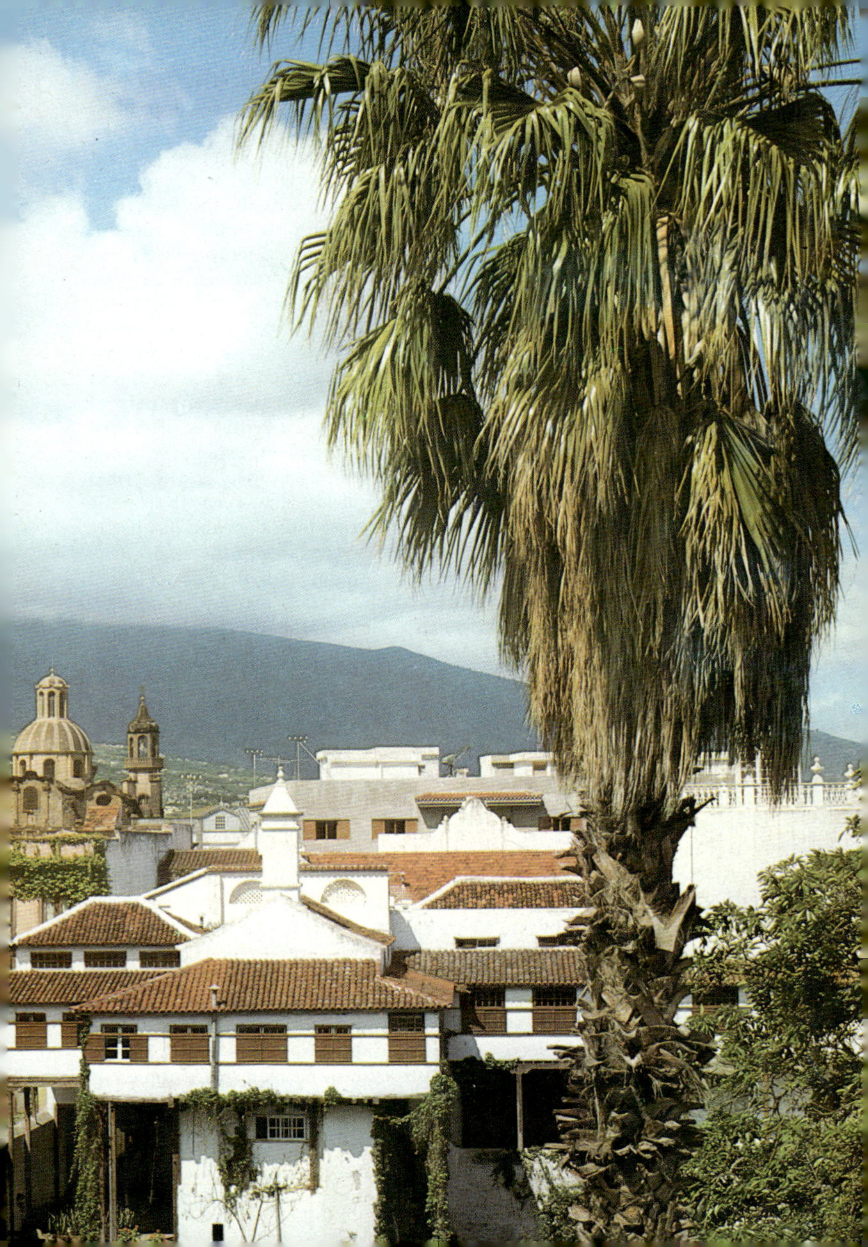

for the Valley of La Orotava has a grandeur that is seldom equalled, and in the days when the wandering scientific baron visited it must have been even more beautiful than now. Largely bordered by high peaks, it extends like a gigantic, gently sloping green tapestry, from the foot of the mountains to the sea. In the background is the majesty of the Teide, at times with its colossal structure without the least veil, at others girt with a belt of clouds. Sea and peak unite thanks to the beautiful brightly coloured tapestry which changes its tonality, becoming slightly darker until it joins the blue of the ocean, as if another inland sea, a green one, were mating with the Atlantic.

It the centre of the valley, La Orotava is an ancient urban group of old mansions which housed the nobility of the island in times past and preserves much of its character. Other times arrived and the lordliness of La Orotava has gradually melted away as it has become part of our epoch, though the illustrious farmer remains, the cultivator of memories and bananas. Old palaces, carefully preserved by those who dwell in them, display their balconies in the intricate Canary style, with grilles and lattices carved of dark woods, while inside they keep the family parchments and honour their memory. The agricultural wealth has partly gone to change into tourist wealth, and the descendants of the landowners of olden days vary the working of their estates with that of the hotel industry, where they give evidence of their «fair play» and activity. In La Orotava there are craftsmen's guilds of real worth, and the wood carving, ornamentation and high class furniture are all good. At the beginning of summer, on the day of Corpus Christi, the streets where the procession is to pass are covered with beautiful tapestries made of flowers; this work is offered to the Supreme Being who, as He passes, destroys the patterns and reproductions of works of art eagerly constructed with petals by the hands of those who are both artists and believers. The carpets of flowers of La Orotava are famous, as are those of La Laguna, where this offering to the Lord is also made.

A few kilometres towards the sea is the port of La Cruz, the first and principal tourist centre in the Canaries. What in past centuries was simply the port of La Cruz de La Orotava, the region's outlet to the sea, a place of commercial agents from several countries and for the leisure of the people of the valley, has become a thriving city in which numerous hotels, inns and hostels mix with night clubs, restaurants, typical taverns, snack-bars and discothèques. No less than twenty thousand foreigners, relieved at regular intervals, reside in Puerto de La Cruz, which has modified its old structures and managed to preserve its typical districts and features of its past life in spite of constructing broad streets, most of which run into the crowded Avenida de Colón

La Orotava preserves important traces of popular Canary architecture.

La Orotava. Church of the Conception. High altar.

Preparing the carpets of flowers and different kinds of earth in their natural colours, for the feast of Corpus Christi in La Orotava.

La Orotava. Town Hall.

Puerto de la Cruz. Partial aspect of the Artificial Lake and its united, César Manrique work. ▶

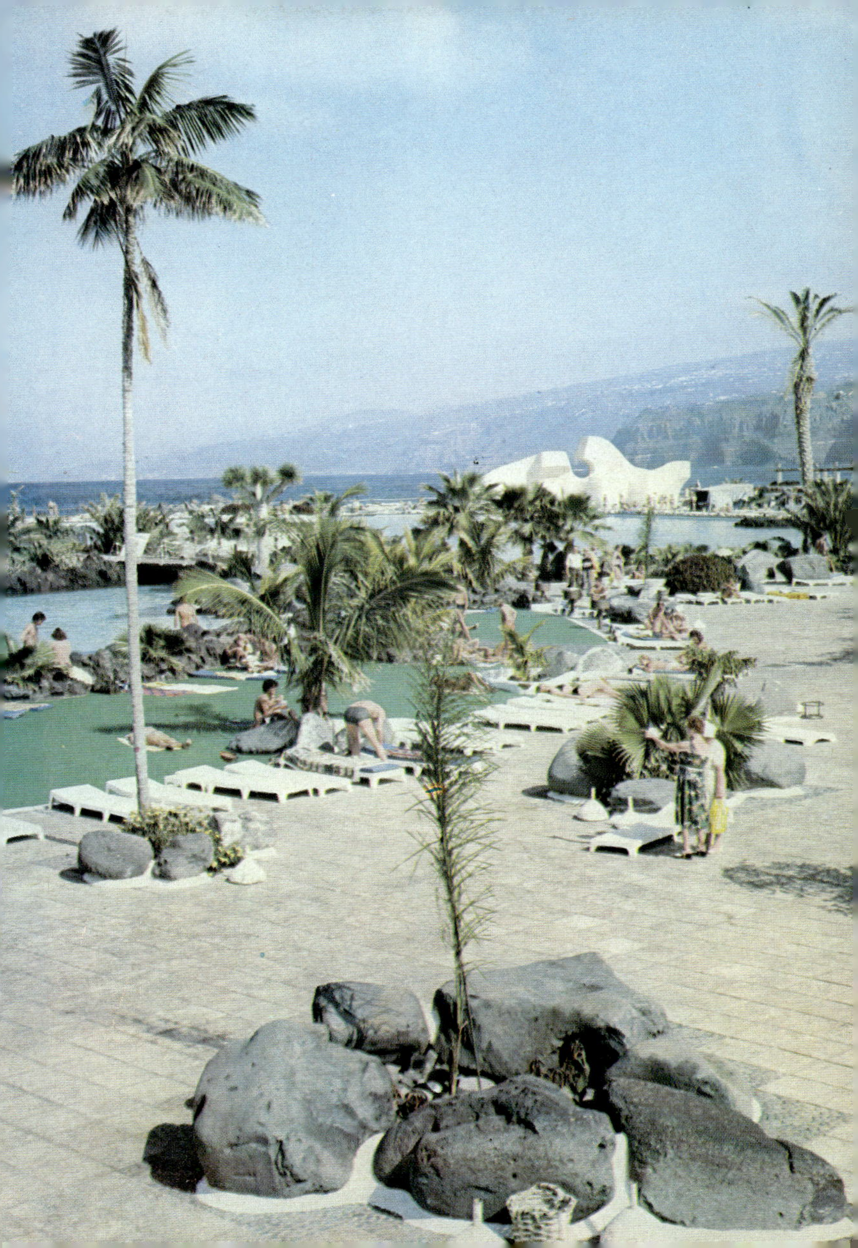

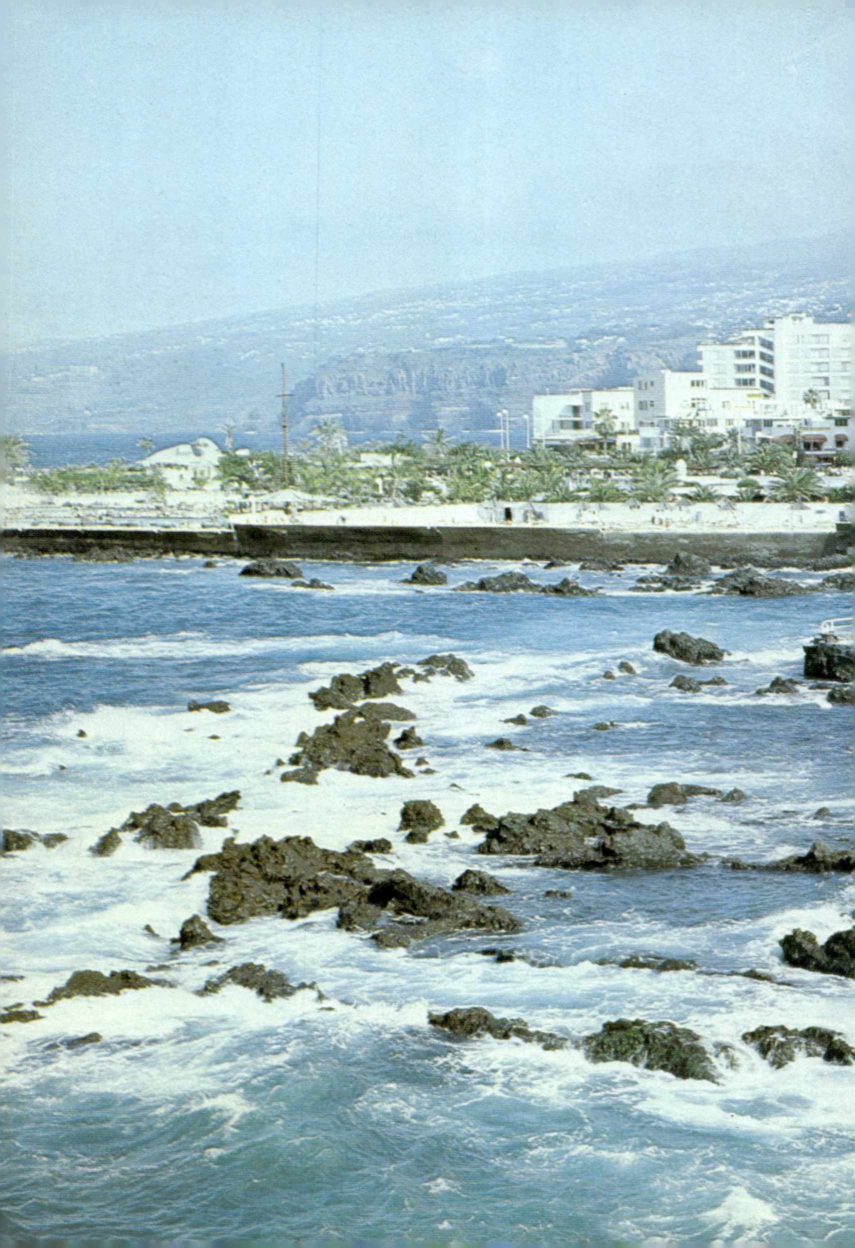

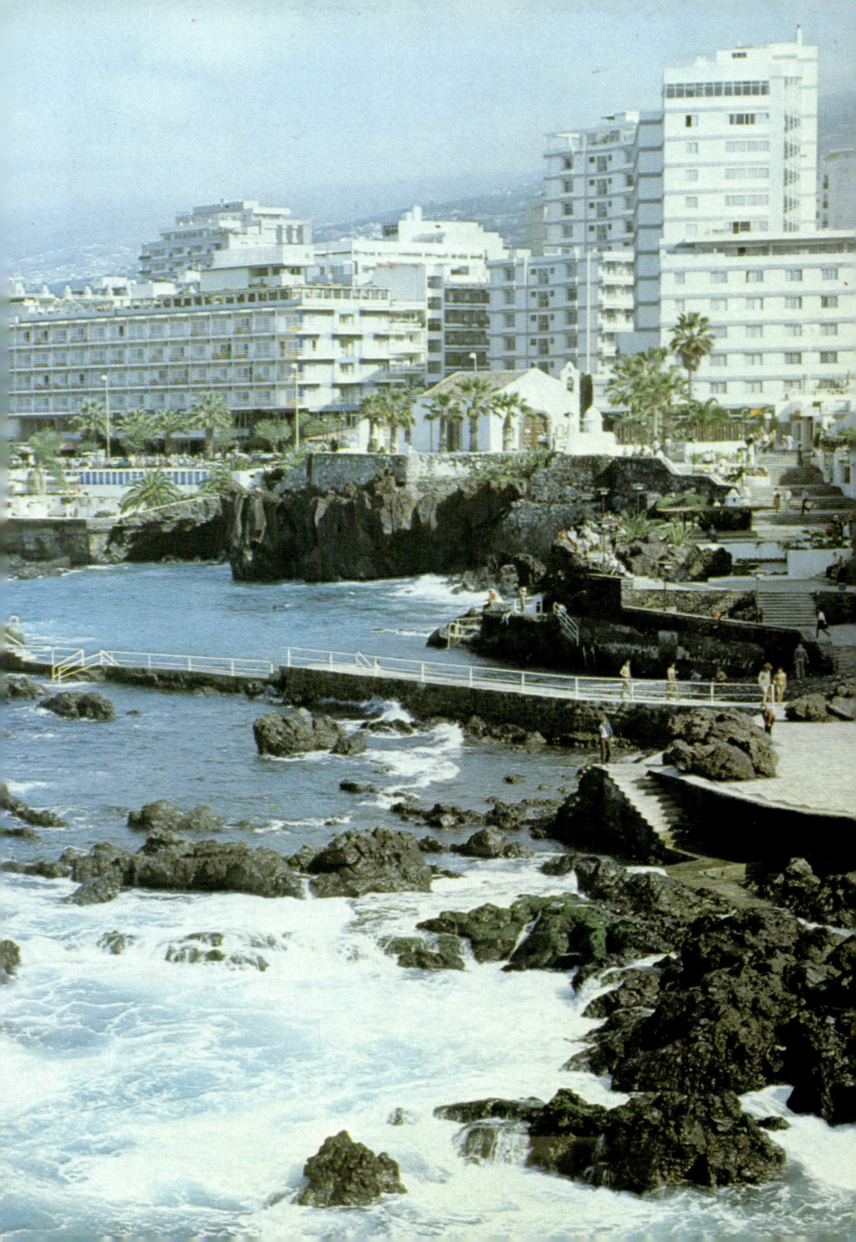

Indoor swimming pools of a big hotel of the Puerto de la Cruz.

◀ Another aspect of the renowned Puerto de la Cruz.

which runs by the sea shore. The Martiánez beach of clear dark sand continues the coastline from the port, and is then transformed into beautifully made lakes and open-air swimming pools, amusement centres and sports zones. The comfortably warm climate, the sun and the scarcity of wind are important attractions of the Port; without forgetting its past, its present is smiling and so splendid that it captivates the visitor. From very early till very late, languages from all Europe and even from more distant countries are heard in its streets, avenues, beaches and swimming pools, spoken by pretty blondes and corpulent Nordics mingled with red-cheeked English and chattering French. Perhaps one of the attractions of Puerto de la Cruz that are most appreciated is supplied by its visitors themselves, who are not in any way, we may say in passing, members of the tourist type with guitar slung round the neck, horrible clothing and slender purse.

Puerto de la Cruz is not too expensive. It can even be economical, but the visitor who lives by begging or on bread and a tin of sardines has kept clear of it.

The old pier and the little beach retain a typical note. The fishermen are still there in their white boats named after virgins or saints, or at most recall their wife or daughter; they come back at dawn with a shining cargo of Atlantic fish. There is the bronzed girl with the golden hair talking to the swarthy sea-wolf; they exchange cigarettes and carry out small commercial operations which end with a bag in which she carries off half a dozen fresh fish or some succulent shellfish. At night Puerto de la Cruz is lit up and very lively. The centres of attraction, the hotel grills, the swimming pools, fill with people out for amusement. There is music, there are high class variety turns, whisky alternates with the wines of the country and the fragrant products of Andalusia. The Puerto, as the Tinerfeños call it for short, becomes the centre and beacon of the island. Meanwhile the quiet, elegant hotels, at a certain distance but not too far from the bustle, look after the people who seek silence and want to forget great cities, and next morning go for a walk, a dip or a sunbathe, accompanied by a good book; there is the right place for everyone in Puerto de la Cruz.

In silence the old castle of San Felipe, sentinel of bygone epochs, on guard against pirates, contemplates the city, gazing at the old chapel of St. Telmo, in a silent dialogue of memory of past adventures and ancient devotions.

Artificial Lake and swimming pools of the hotels in the Puerto de la Cruz.

Aspect of the Acclimation Botanical Garden of la Orovata, founded in the XVIII century, with the initiative of Don Alonso de Nava and Benítez de Lugo, marquis of Villanueva del Prado.

VI

THE BOTANICAL GARDEN

In 1788 or 1790, an eminent Tinerfeño, Alonso de Nava y Benítez de Lugo, Marquis of Villanueva del Prado, charged several naturalists and expert gardeners with the formation and care of a garden, which besides plants typical of the Canaries should gather the greatest possible number of flora from all over the world. Thus the Botanical Garden was born, now called the Garden of Acclimatization, dependent on the leading administrative body of the province, the Municipal Council. In the Botanical, as it is popularly called, the most varied examples of the island flora may be seen close to rare and striking specimens of the vegetable world of distant countries. A visit to the Botanical is a must for the interested visitor who wants to know thoroughly the country he is visiting.

Gorse, rosemary, araucarias, Canary pines, heather, *fayas* and *tejinastes* intermingle, in ordered disorder, with *tabaibas* and prickly pears, chestnuts, *balos* and fuller's teasels. Presiding over everythying, by right, is the dragon tree, that strange and curious object which exists only in the islands and is no other than a living fossil, a memory of the vegetation of the Secondary which, by a caprice of Nature, survives in the Canaries solely as a living document of the remote youth of the planet. Flowers from the Canaries, flowers from the tropics and nearby Africa with those from more distant America, minute plants and gigantic trees and shrubs are to be found here for the admiration of all and for help to the scholar.

VII

THE LOWER ISLAND

Almost in the confines of the Valley of La Orotava, in what formed the boundaries of the old Guanche kingdom or *menceyato* of Taoro, we find Los Realejos, the chief town of an extensive municipality whose fields are complemented by great areas of banana plantations. When we have passed this district and left the valley, we find a road which skirts precipices and offers spots with marvellous views, leading to what is called the «Lower Island». It first passes through San Juan de La Rambla, another very attractive town which first offers the visitor its small, sheltered beach by the hamlet of Las Aguas, with fishermen's

The North coast, with the Socorro beach at Los Realojes in the foreground.

View of Los Realejos, in the Valley of La Orotava.

Banana trees in La Rambla.

View of Las Aguas, on the coast of San Juan de La Rambla.

houses and samll summer and leisure residences. Down below to one side of the road is a narrow strip of more banana plantations stretching to the sea; on the other are high peaks which at times overwhelm the observer with their almost sheer walls, broken from time to time by deep ravines on whose borders there grow a confusion of flowers, bushes and canebrakes. San Juan de la Rambla has a flavour of other days, with narrow cool streets and big houses with gardens behind them. After passing this locality the scenery changes a little, becoming less hilly and more agricultural. Zones of lava, a memory of almost forgotten eruptions, display sharp peaks of a dark colour, and often alternate with farms and orchards constructed by excavating into the rocky soil; like gigantic flower-pots they contain fruit trees and bushes among which the eternal banana is most prominent.

A few kilometres further on is Icod de los Vinos, an important city that begins the Lower Island and is both agricultural and commercial. It is the meeting point for the inland localities distant from the sea; its people work and modernise it while they lovingly preserve the legacy of other generations. Here the beautiful Park of Lorenzo Cáceres contains the oldest and biggest dragon tree in the Canaries. Thousands of years have passed since the enormous tree was born of the earth; in its shade the primitive Guanches must have met in council, and centuries later wise men in sober attire would have met beneath it to discuss the news from Spain brought by the sailing ships that put in at the nearby port of Garachico. Perhaps they talked of events and persons that for them were the latest news, but which after the long passage from the mother country were already out of date. More than one «Te Deum» for the reigning monarch must have been sung in the churches of Tenerife when, many miles away in other Spanish churches, they were saying Latin prayers for the soul of the monarch who had just died.

Icod de Los Vinos, as its name implies, has a plain where many vineyards produce rich wines, light in colour and with a special flavour. Dry and fragrant, dry-sweet and curious, but pleasant to the palate, or sweet and appreciated by ladies with biscuits and cakes, the wines of Icod are clearly distinguishable from the others of the Island.

San Marcos beach, with hotels of various types, caters for tourists in this important city.

Two centuries ago Garachico was an imprtant port which sometimes rivalled that of Santa Cruz. They were its best times, but its prosperity ended abruptly in the early 18th century, when a volcanic eruption in the neighbouring peaks sent down rivers of burning lava and scattered hot ashes. The burning river reached the sea where it died, but it had first devastated Garachico, stopped up its harbour and almost

The palm trees harmonise this rural grouping of Icod de los Vinos. ▶

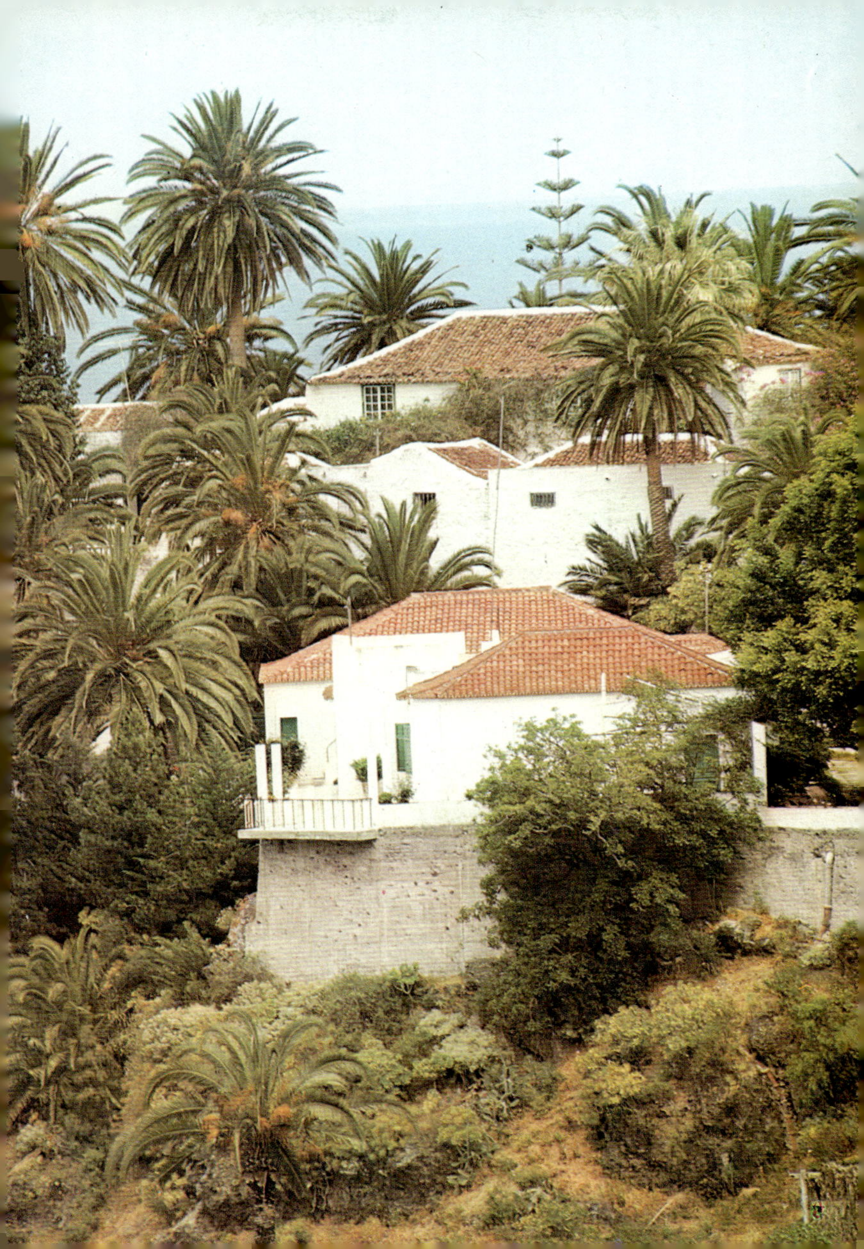

Icod de los Vinos is the town of the Drago.

Icod de los Vinos is also a lordly town.

San Marcos beach, in the municipality of Icod de los Vinos.

San Pedro is a picturesque little village on the Garachico coast.

View of Garachico, surrounded by sea and lava

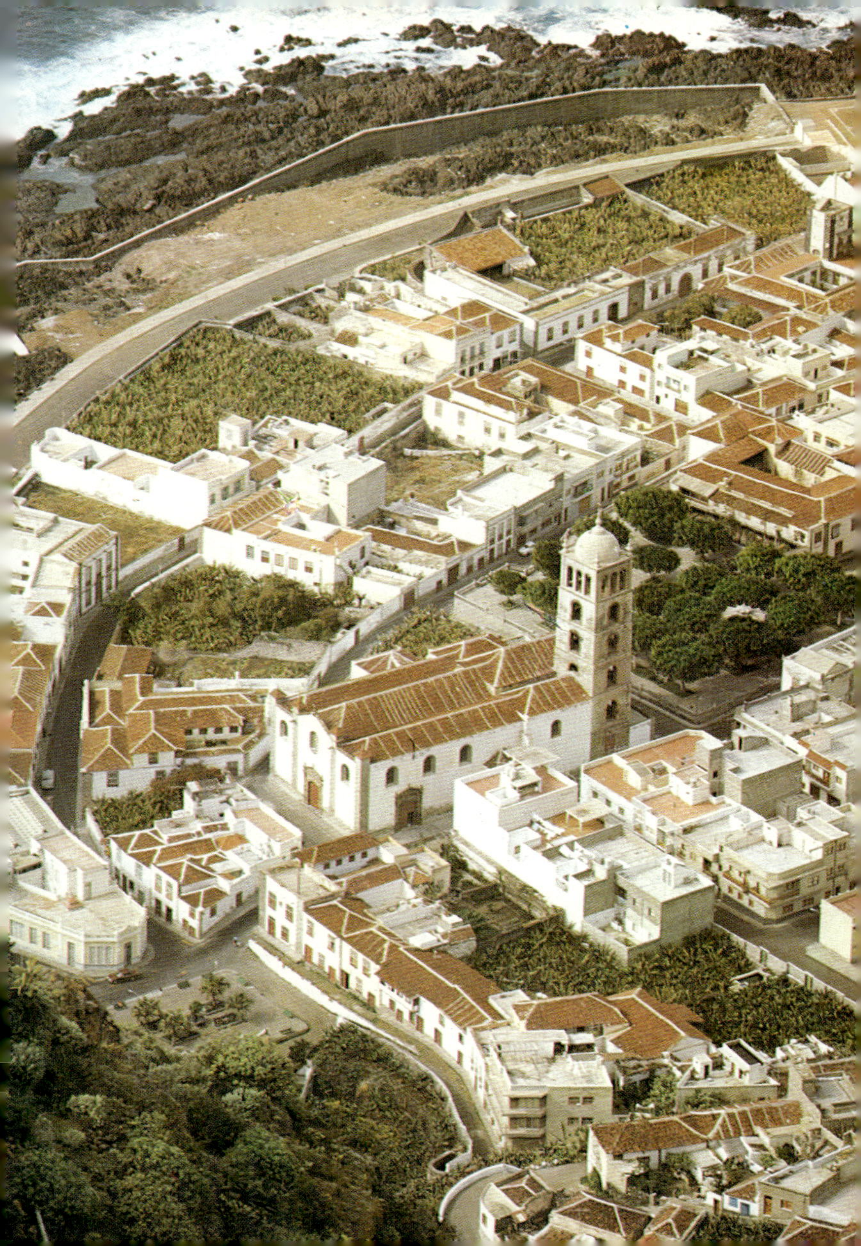

View of the coast of Buenavista del Norte.

The Tanque and Buenavista del Norte.

completely destroyed the locality. Hundreds of people disappeared, sturdy sailing ships were buried by the lava before their crews could put out to sea, and the flourishing town remained hardly more than a memory. Today Garachico is a comparatively important urban nucleus, a farming centre and a holiday resort. Its rough coastline shelters a real paradise for bathers, yachtsmen and fishermen. Old convents and ancient houses recall its epoch of glory.

Los Silos is the last place but one on the route, and also ranks as a Town; it is a pleasant, smiling place, of small area and great beauty. A short distance away is its competitor and sister, Buenavista, a place of farmers and fishermen; this ends the tour of what, without much respect for geography, is called the North.

VIII

WHAT SHOULD NOT BE LEFT BEHIND

If you are travelling in a hurry or have planned a certain route, it becomes necessary to leave aside, if not all that is secondary, at least anything that would prolong your journey. We have therefore left unmentioned some interesting and very beautiful districts. We are going to devote this chapter to places which deserve attention, because if we visit them we can better understand the saying that Tenerife is a continent in miniature.

Let us suppose for a moment that we are still in La Laguna. It is cool there, more so at night, and we must admit that in winter it is really cold. We already know its plain and have enjoyed the peace of its walks and roads; but now we are going to make some trips that are not very long but very attractive. We may decide on two opposite directions and, after a short examination of the possibilities, decide on a route, that to Hidalgo Point. But it will first be necessary, if we want to look at beautiful spots, to stop on the mountain and then compare it with the coast. Following the road to Tejina, straight as an arrow and adorned with tall eucalyptus, we reach the crossroads of Las Canteras. Here the road forks and ceases to be straight. To the right it climbs towards the mountain of Las Mercedes, while to the left it drops towards Tegueste, Tejina and Bajamar, to end at La Punta. The distance is not far, and may therefore permit the visitor to climb the mountain. The road soon enters some dense and pleasant woods, winding higher and higher while the temperature becomes cooler

The spinal mountain range and the Teide, from Las Mercedes mountain.

The rugged coast of Taganana in the northern part of the island.

and we fill our lungs with pleasure. Suddenly a little plain, bounded by high rocky walls, claims our attention. This is the Plain of Los Viejos, a shady, enchanting place; at the end of it we can see, from above, plenty of cool water. A good place for a stop, where many tourists like to eat a snack and refresh their mouth with the pure water from the running fountain. There are several fenced-off areas where mufflon, and other species with which it has been decidad to restock the island with big game, are acclimatised. Beyond the height, we still climb until we reach the Cross of the Carmen, situated on a rough semiplateau. There was can restore our strength with tasty island dishes chiefly based on rabbit «al salmorejo» and, strangely enough, with fresh fish brought by steep paths from Taganana, a lovely fishing village a thousand metres lower and a dozen kilometres away; until some Years ago it was difficult to get to. Now the new road by El Bailadero enables us to reach by car.

The mountain of Las Mercedes stretches as far as the Anaga peninsula. *Aceviños,* laurels, *laurisilvas, fayas* and heather mark the heights of the extensive forest, and there are thickets on the highest points. Going down towards Anaga, there are little mountain villages such as Las Batanes and Las Carboneras in clearings, the home of independent farmers, hunters who sometimes poach and are always enthusiastic, and, from time to time when the body calls, fishermen who march for many hours before they reach the coast.

On what is called the Peak of the Englishman, perhaps in memory of an important traveller from the British Isles, there is a belvedere from which we can gaze at the magnificent panorama, with views of both sides of the island at its narrowest part.

Returning again and going towards Las Canteras, we may continue by the downhill road. On either side of it are trees and orchards in another immense valley with peaks at its sides. We first pass the little village of Pedro Alvarez, where the people grow potatoes, vegetables and fruit trees; two kilometres farther on is Tegueste, a small municipal enclave between the two «great ones» of La Laguna and Santa Cruz. Its Council has always managed to maintain itself between the cities which at times keep up a friendly struggle. Tegueste if famous for its wines and artichokes, its almonds and pears and for something else, the toughness of its men who are keen on the regional sport of wrestling in which their strength and style has often brought them vicory. The road continues to descend and soon passes through Tejina, where a side road leads to Tacoronte, mentioned previously, crossing the rich agricultural lands of the Guerra Valley. Tejina is scarcely thee kilometres from Bajamar, a former fishing village which started years ago to be a summer resort for the middle classes of La Laguna, and then soon

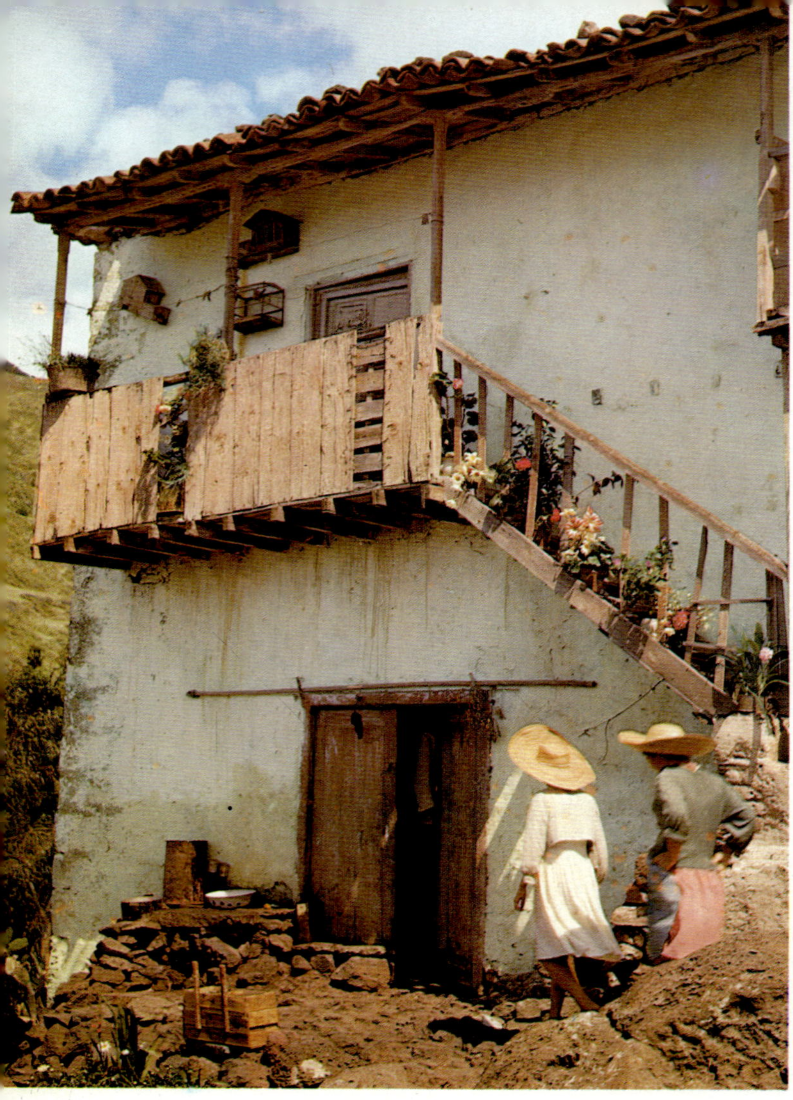

Towards the coast to the West of La Laguna, Tejina and the Valley of Guerra.

To the North East of the Valley of Guerra, in the same municipality of La Laguna, Punta del Hidalgo and Bajamar are a first-class tourist attraction.

became a first class tourist centre with good hotels, amusements and modern houses; it reaches as far as Hidalgo Point, an old district of seamen who, like many other Tinerfeños, divide their attention between the net and the oar and the hoe. Their rugged cliffs now house a tourist population worth taking into account. Like nearly all the island, the district is closely hemmed in between the sea and the mountain. On a mountain with twin peaks the legend of «The Two Brothers» was woven, which tells of impossible loves and weddings where death was present. Tejina, like Bajamar and the Point, still maintains some sugar cane plantations, which in other centuries were its chief source of riches. Old sugar mills and primitive stills have made way for hotels with several stars and a snack-bar, but the sugar plantations still remain, as does an important distillery of *aguardientes* and liquors; it produces qualities to which many can bear witness.

This is an excursion that can be made in a few hours, like the other previously mentioned which also starts from La Laguna and leads to places of great beauty.

It is worth going to La Esperanza, another high mountain zone, more extensive than that of Las Mercedes. We may first visit Aguagarcía, a picturesque district half mountain and half tilled land, and then go

The Mount of the Esperanza, with its great pinewoods, stands out on the spinal mountain range.

The Roques and the Teide. ▶

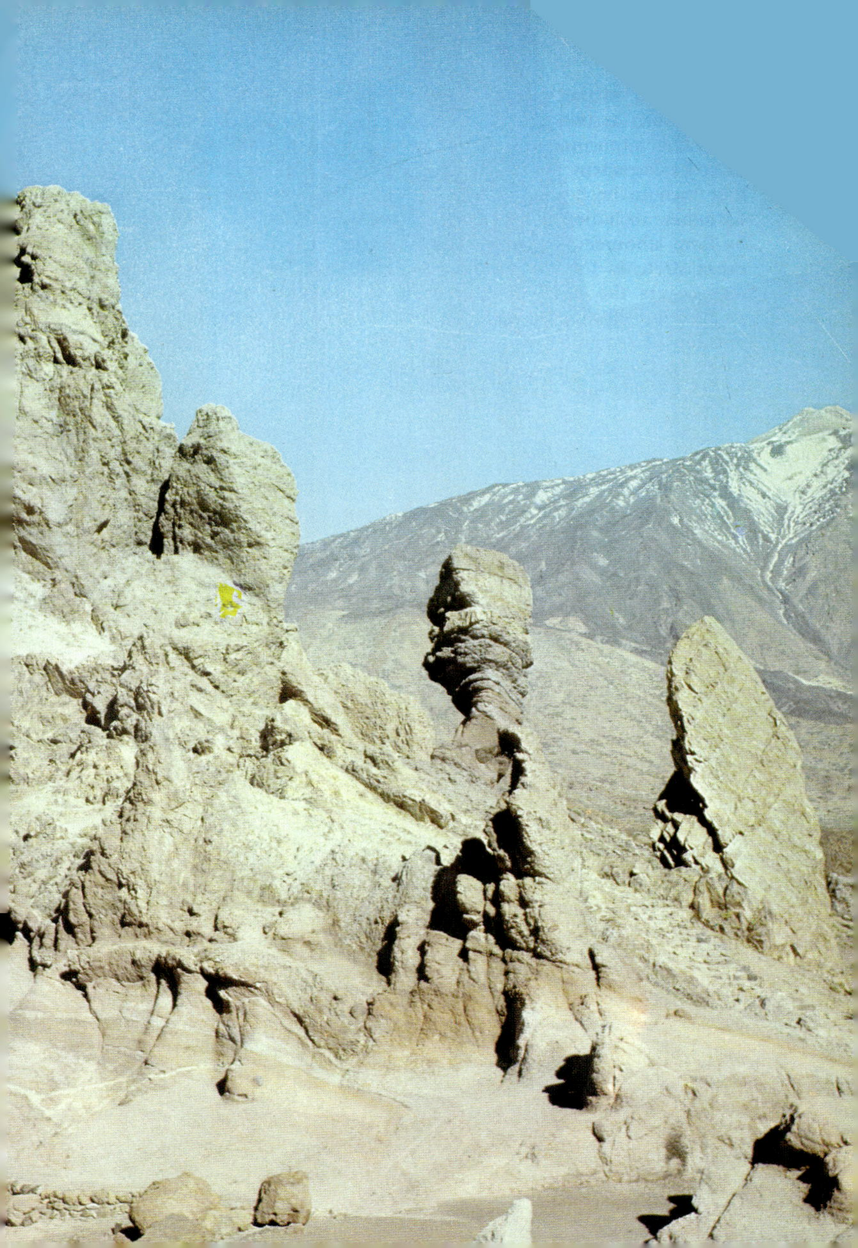

village of La Esperanza, the birthplace of popular
of «un variscacillo apenas» (hardly a tap) to play
ce of the blow with an ash staff they have given
person, hard enough for him to be carried off by
aled; it also preserves ancient customs and peasant
g the local cloak, a covering used all over the island
, shepherds and wayfarers. The mountain of La Espe-
r many kilometres, climbs and reaches the vegetation
that co   peaks giving access to the Teide. It was in one of
its clearings that the Spanish National Movement was born; this historic
meeting is remembered by a monolith erected at Las Raíces. If we
continue we may reach Las Cañadas and even the foot of the Teide,
but this is another matter and we shall refer to it in another chapter.

IX

LAS CAÑADAS AND THE TEIDE PEAK

We can get to Las Cañadas by the road along the spine of the
mountains, a work of military origin in the hard years of the second

Two aspects of Las Cañadas, in the massif of the Teide.

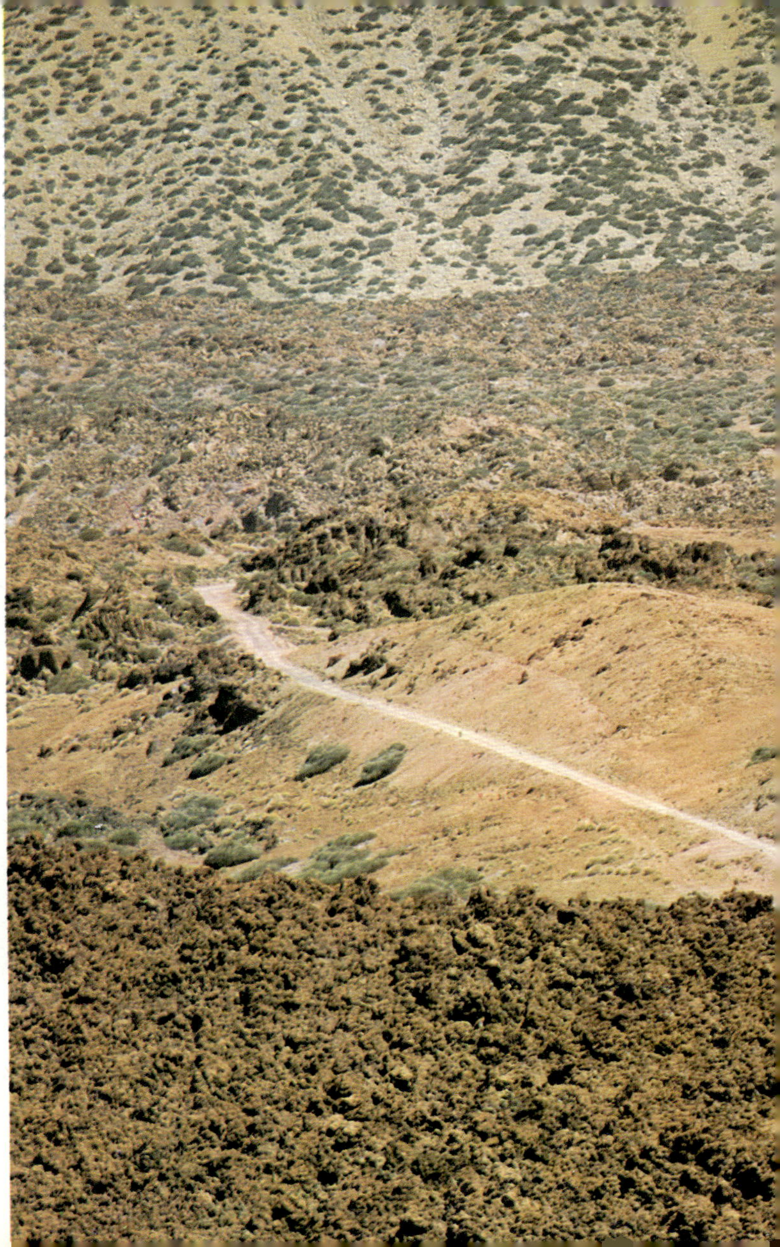

The Plain of Ucanca is a sea of petrified lava.

The Teide dominates the whole landscape.

world war. The road to La Esperanza joins up with this road, which at times runs along the very edge of the gigantic mountain which forms the whole island. Another practical route starts from La Orotava, climbs up with many bends to the wooded zone of Aguamansa and continues climbing up to Portillo de la Villa, a kind of pass which suddenly comes out before the grand circle of the Teide.

Las Cañadas, which crown the island, are an unusual crater caused by fabulous geological convulsions in remote times; the Teide rises in the middle of them, its peak standing out above the other high peaks that surround the great circle. Hard basalt rocks, tortured lands in which the lava of old eruptions solidified in the strangest forms, imitating fabulous dragons, zones covered with volcanic scoria and ashes, pozzolanic lands, stones of dark and bright obsidian, phenoliths, sulphur, compose the zone which is slightly circular in shape with a diameter of more than twelve kilometres. The landscape is imposing as a whole and strange in its ever different details. The colours vary from the brilliant white of the snows and sands to the black of obsidian, passing through bluish stony formations, reddish clefts as if hewn by a giant's sword, with the greenish tones of phenoliths and the yellowish ones of sulphur showing at different points. In winter everything is hidden by the mantle of snow, and the heavy falls smooth out the wrinkles and seem to lessen the tremendous hardness of the land. Here and there are patches of broom and the *tajinastes* which produce spots of bright colour in spring. The fauna, as if impressed by the majesty of the heights, is scarce and silent, for silence is one of the characteristics of Las Cañadas. A certain little bird peculiar to the place, known as the Teide Bird, an occasional hawk or small eagle and some rabbits are almost the only beings endowed with movement that live there; it looks as if the Universe, in a tremendous convulsion, in an instant, had been petrified at the command of a higher being.

The circle of Las Cañadas, besides its stone formations, has broad approach routes where the great wall has been broken. The woods replace the stone and the dominant colour in the scene is green. There are forests of giant pines, like those of Vilaflor, the highest point in the island, some 1,400 metres above sea level. Compact masses of broom and heather; cedars of Lebanon, recently acclimatised thanks to an ambitious reafforestation plan, carpet the surface of the earth and between them, at times even emphasising its individualism among compact lava formations, shows the note of colour, paradoxically humble and arrogant at the same time, of the Teide violet.

There are some zones in which the spectacle is so grand, so different from others, that they have been described as «lunar landscapes»; now that our natural satellite has been trodden by human feet, and human

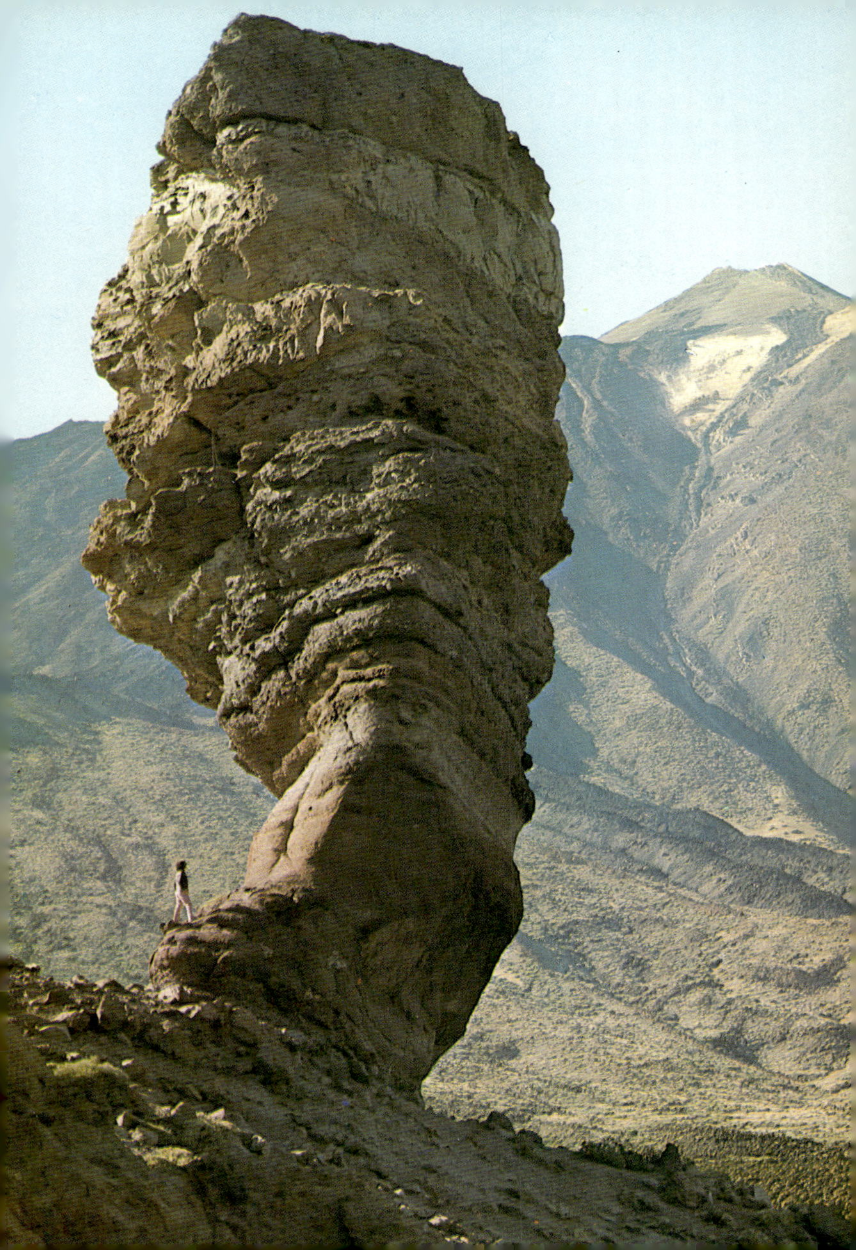

Los Roques and the Teide compose this singular scene.

«Tajinastes» flourishing in Las Cañadas

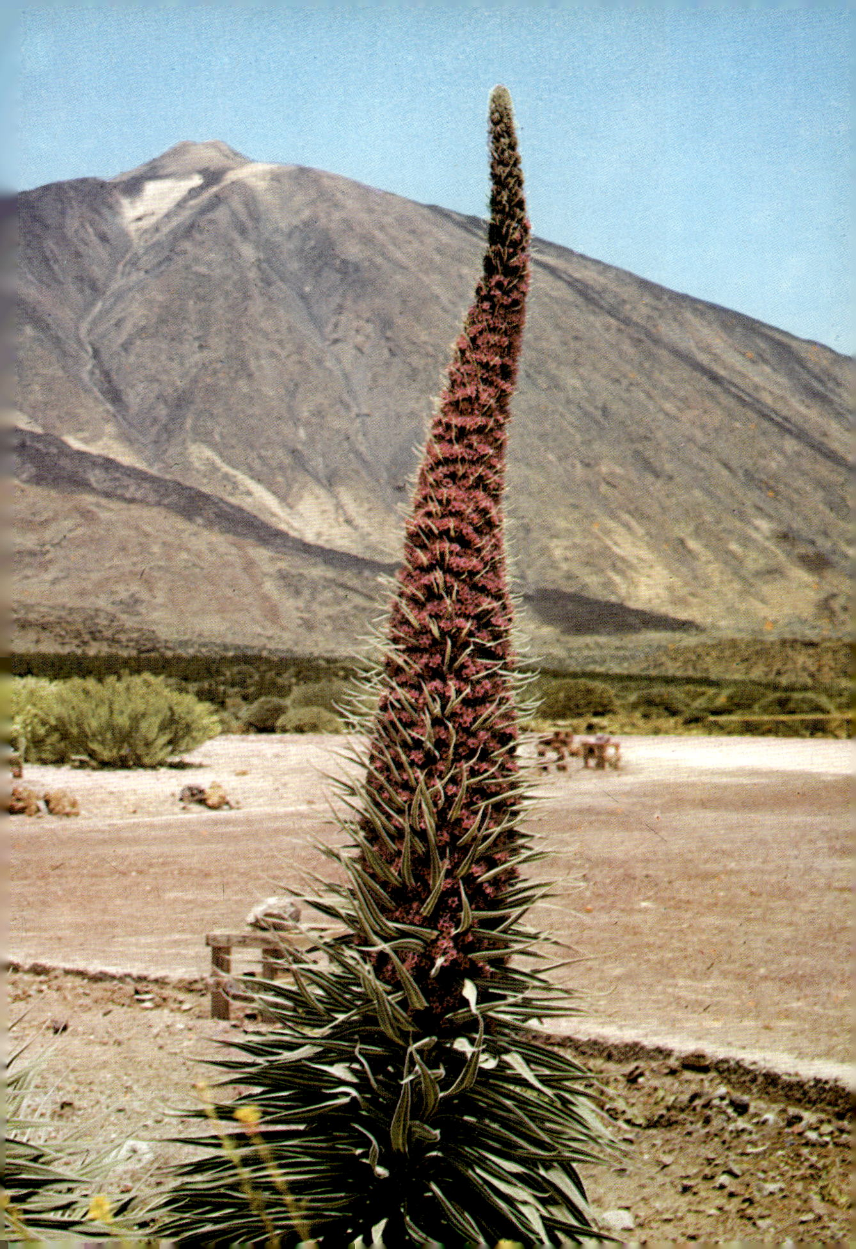

eyes have been able to marvel at it without the need for great telescopes, we may state as a fact that some parts of the Teide and Las Cañadas do not seem to belong to our planet.

Dominating it all, in majesty, is the great volcano, the peak that looks on to all the islands of the Archipelago whence it can be seen on clear days, which navigators make out before anything else as a proof that thet are near the islands, the Teide.

The peak of the Teide is alkost conical in shape, in the classical style of a volcano; though it has been sleeping for centuries, its past eruptions have been recorded. The last on record occurred in the late 17th century. The volcano seems decided to leave such tasks to its smaller brothers; so the last eruption recorded in the island was nearly seventy years ago, entrusted, so to speak, to another crater on the height of the neighbouring mountain of Chahorra, which affected the high zones of Garachico without its effects being dangerous or unduly devastating. At the top of the peak the crater yawns, peaceful and half stopped up, although some chimneys remain which recall epochs of great activity. The thought is terrifying of the tremendous geological convulsions which shaped Las Cañadas, as it is terrifying to imagine the eruptions that occurred millenia ago, in the youth of the volcano.

Now, eternal snows pile up in the hollow of the crater and the winter rains shelter in rocky formations from the hot canicular breezes. In winter a white mantle coveres the enormous cone 3,718 metres above the sea, and all the other peaks which seem to render homage to it; the Old Peak, Chahorra, the Sombrerito (Little Hat) of Chasna, White Mountain, etc., all of them about three thousand metres high. The Cañadas are also covered with snow, and the flat zones such as the beautiful Ucanca and Maja; the smooth slopes of the glens that give access are magnificent places for skiing.

A tourist Parador with all modern conveniences and comfort, an astrophysical observatory, a high mountain shelter and the television antennae and transmitters are the only buildings in the zone, declared a natural park and so protected that it may preserve its original aspect without the hand of man changing what was arranged by Nature. In our days the ascent of the Teide Peak may be made in the comfortable, safe cabins of a cableway which was installed little more than a year ago.

The Old Peak, on the South East flank of the Teide.

The modern funicular on the Teide.

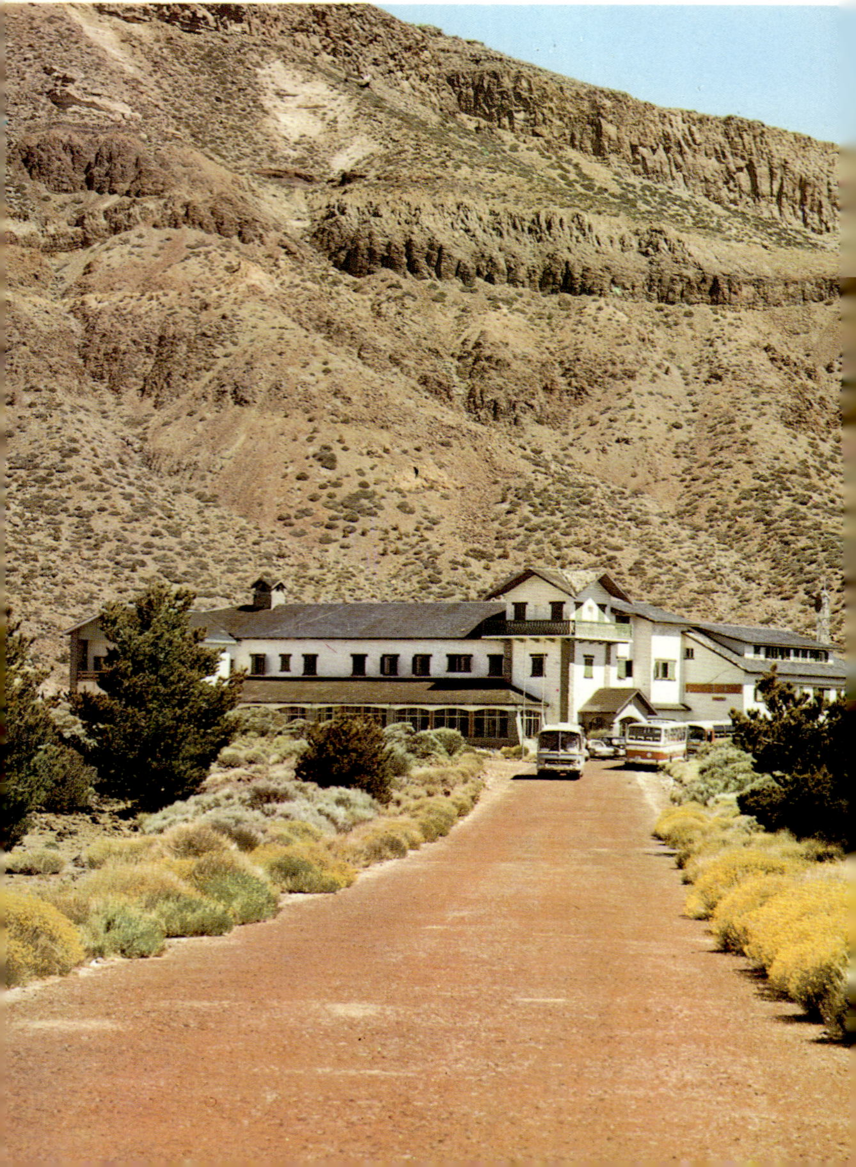

Vilaflor is the municipality nearest to the Teide; its capital is 1,400 metres high.

The National Tourist Parador at Las Cañadas del Teide stands at the foot of Mount Guajara.

On the South coast, Los Cristianos has become an important tourist centre

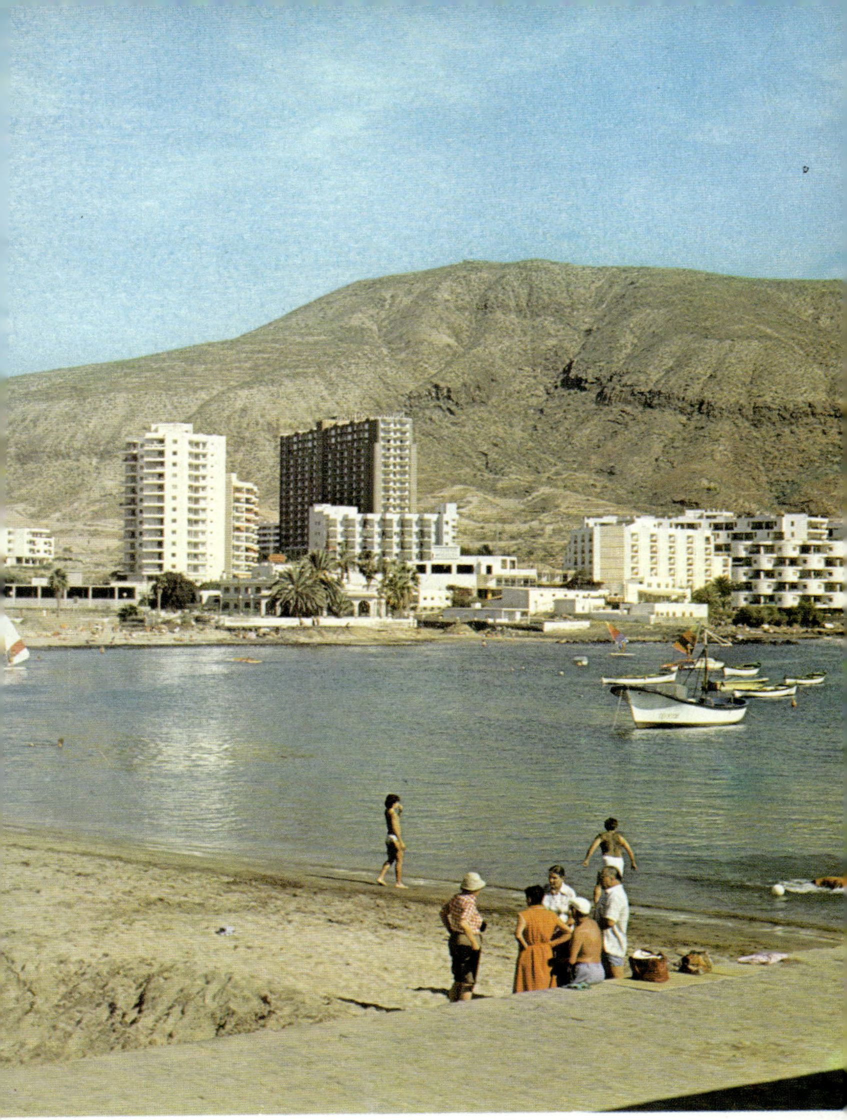

X

THE AMPLE SOUTH

Whereas the northern coast of Tenerife is rugged, with coves and little capes, with valleys and slopes covered with verdure in which water sings and man has made gardens, the southern and south-eastern coasts seem to belong to another continent, or at least to a country thousands of kilometres away. Very dry, with great plains and open valleys, the ground is whitish, greyish and sometimes dark. The land in the south is dotted with stones, tufas, sands and ashes of lava. Here and there valleys sheltered from the winds or zones more favoured with the appearance of water, which is eagerly sought in the bowels of the earth, vary the landscape and form oases of vegetation which supply splendid fruit and large yields. The earth is rich in spite of its dryness, and easily agrees to return a hundred for one.

The relative immensity of the south of Tenerife surprises us, makes us catch our breath, especially if we compare it with the other side of the island. Even the people seem different for they are more serious, leaner, but yet more welcoming, as if the difficulties of their daily struggle with Nature made them come closer to human beings in order to console and help themselves.

The South, however, is undergoing a great transformation. Water, a basic element in the islands, already reaches nearly all districts and through a wide system of canals, made with great efforts and a lot of money, is converting into gardens what were formerly desert and stony ground. A peculiar system of cultivation, thought up to save water and spread irrigation, may often be observed. Potatoes and tomatoes, which were nearly always the genuine products of the South, grow in strange white, heavy earth, different from others we know. It is the tufa, a kind of very porous volcanic gravel, which is spread in a layer of a few centimetres over the dark reddish earth in which the seeds are to germinate. This layer of tufa ensures the aeration and at the same time fulfils a more important mission: to make the moisture last longer. In the last few years many zones have been opened up to the crop which is king of the islands: the banana. As in other places, they worked long and hard, they brought the rich black earth from the high ground, sometimes more than seventy kilometres, and constructed colossal «flower-pots» which cover hectares and hectares, so that the banana tree could flourish arrogantly, which is here sheltered from exceptional winds and grows readily, producing a splendid yield.

At the same time, complexes and developments for tourists have been springing up in what not many years ago were lonely and dried-up

Ten-Bel urbanisation corner. Coast of Silence, at the south of the island. ▶

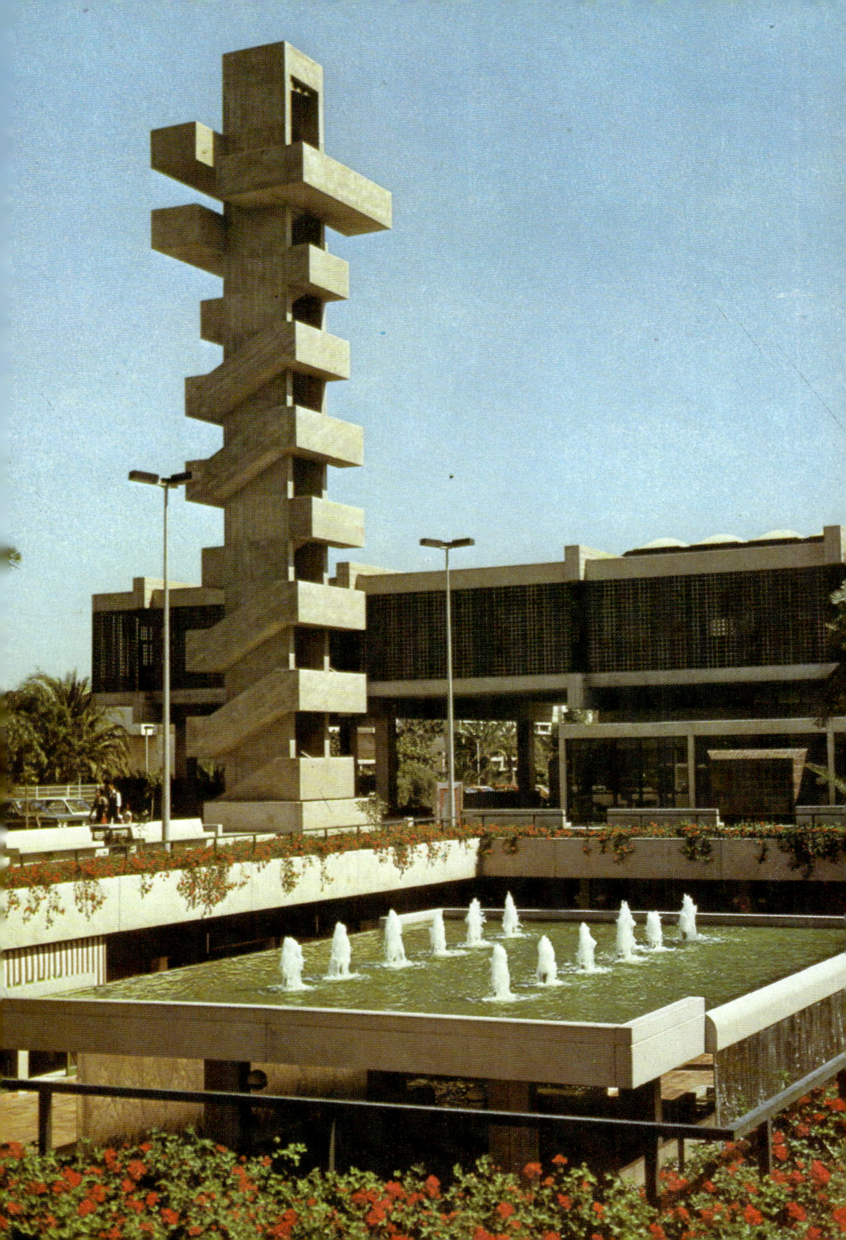

Prickly pears, cacti, hybiscus..., an example of the riches of the flora in the Canaries.

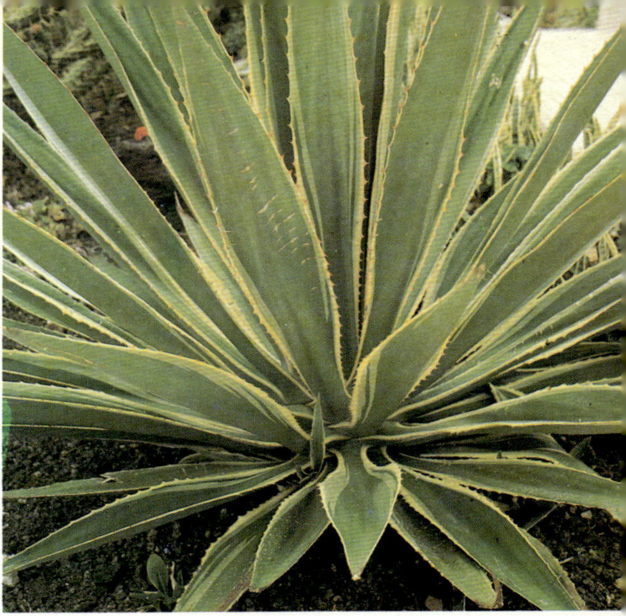

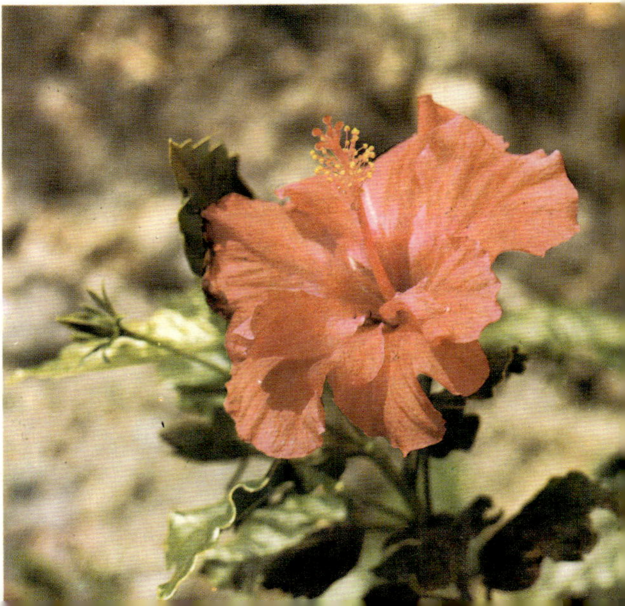

areas: modern and elegant facilities, next to beaches with lighter coloured sand than in the North, sheltered from sea winds, house thousands of visitors, Zones like the Coast of Silence, Beach of the Americas, Los Cristianos, Médano and Chayofa are crowded centres for Tinerfeños and foreigners, amid the gardens with plants of the region, palm trees, shady groves and flowers, always flowers.

XI

FROM SANTA CRUZ TO LOS CRISTIANOS

«Going to the South», as they said years ago, was something like a journey to another country, distant and uncomfortable. An old road, narrow and full of curves, skirting precipices and crossing ravines thanks to daring bridges, crawling round estates whose owners were unaccomodating as to the line of the road, put this part of the island in communication with the capital, which was only reached after hours and hours of tiring journey. There were Tinerfeños who had never trodden this part of the island, and many others who hardly went there once or twice in their life. It was a far-off world which was spoken of as if it were at an enormous distance. At present a straight modern motorway enables us to pass in an hour what used to take five, six or seven, passing and repassing ravines that made people sick, getting round dangers and skidding round curves.

From Santa Cruz to Los Cristianos in one hour: it seems like a miracle! However, it has been achieved and now the Tinerfeños spend their days of fiesta on the beaches of the south, dance in the «boite» of a modern hotel, go underwater fishing in the hours between when they left work and dinner time, coming and going from the South in a short time. Taking the motorway from Santa Cruz, it takes a few minutes to pass the industrial zone, the oil refinery, the warehouses and workshops; in ten minutes we reach the first important tourist centre of Las Caletillas, where hotels, bungalows and villas rise near numerous swimming pools and a pleasant beach. Two kilometres farther on is Candelaria, the first locality of the South. There we find the sanctuary of the Patron Saint of the Archipelago, of the devotion of the Tinerfeños and Canary Islanders in general. A great basilica at the end of a large square by the sea houses the Virgin of Calendaria (Candlemas). The church is majestic and enriched by valuable frescoes by famous artists. The image of Our Lady is very beautiful, and near it are the votive offerings that have been presented to the Queen of Heaven for centuries.

The Basilica of our Lady of Candlemas.

The Patron Saint of the Canaries ▶

A detail of the Basilica of Candlemas.

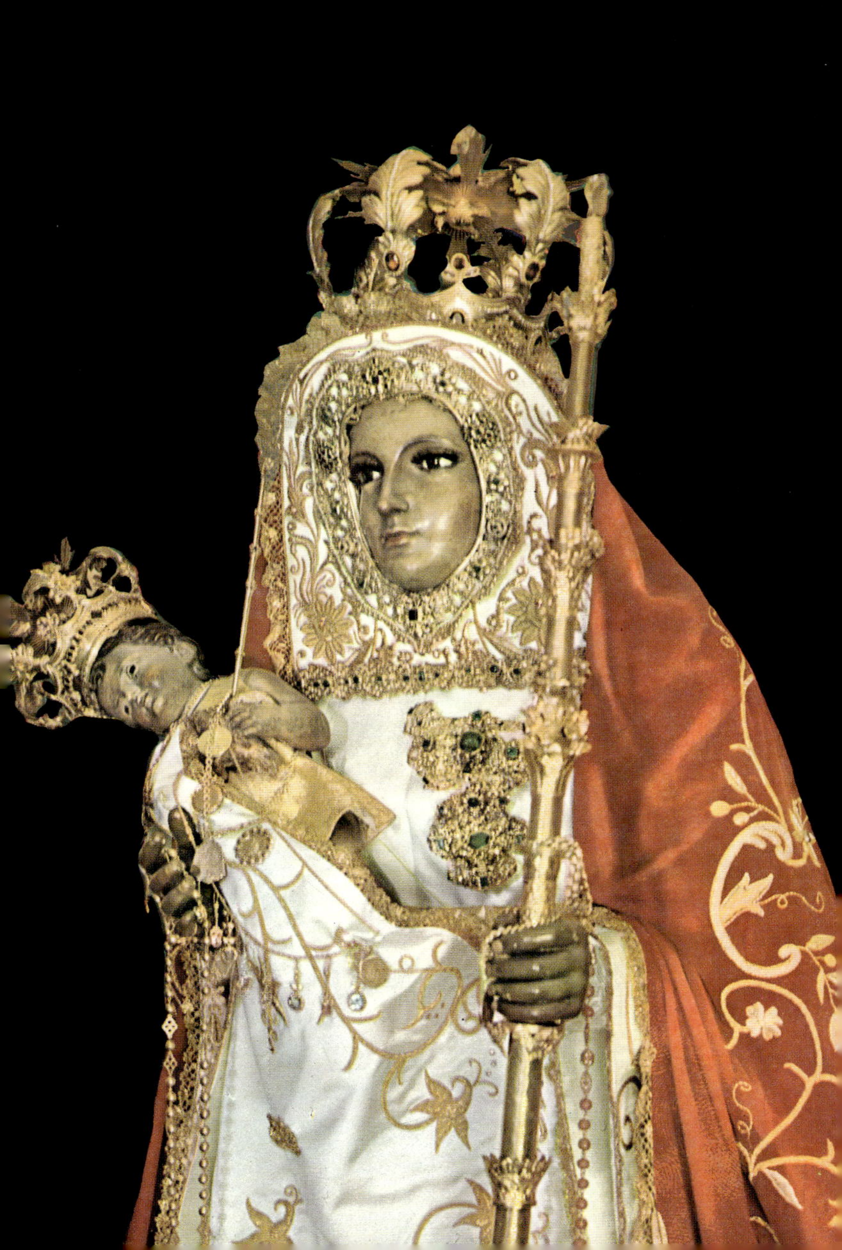

The chronicles tell that an image of the Virgin was brought by the waves to the shore of Candelaria. There the Guanches, half amazed and half frightened, gazed at the celestial apparition which, standing erect, seemd to speak to them. They tried to stone it, but their raised arms were paralyzed until, convinced that they were before someting miraculous, they prostrated themselves in adoration. The image was taken by the aborigines to a nearby cave, where it was worshipped. Later, when the island had been conquered by the Spaniards, the humble cave was transformed into a chapel, and later still into a small church which a few years later was replaced by a great basilica.

Near Candelaria, though to get there we must leave the car and take a secondary road, is Arafo, the producing centre of much appreciated white wines, and the thriving agricultural district of Igueste.

The motorway goes on through the lava zones of the so-called «malpais», interrupted by areas where tobacco, tomatoes and vines are the chief crops; then, almost without transition, it enters the rich valley of Guimar, with one of the most important localities in the South, ranking as a City and with about 18,000 inhabitants. It is a commercial centre, with exporting and industrial firms, Pleasant in design and appearance, it is some three kilometres from the coast, and continues as a built-up area to the Puertito de Guimar, the Tinerfeño name for a little port. The Puertito contains hotels and holiday houses, as well as a little quay for yachts; it is a great place for amateur fisohermen as its neighbouring waters are very well stocked.

Eminently agricultural localities are linked by secondary and branch roads to the motorway, and lie to either side of it. The views of La Medida, El Escobonal, Fasnia, Arisco Viejo and Arico Nuevo, La Cisnera, El Río, Chimiche, and Las Vegas are interesting. From Arico a roads leads off to Poris de Abona, an old landing-place for coastal vessels with a crowded beach and a fishing quay. Farther on and also joined by road to the motorway is Granadilla de Abona, the capital of the district, an important agricultural and commercial centre with some fine buildings and attractive corners. From Granadilla we can go by road to the neighbouring villages of San Miguel, El Roaue and Arona.

The motorway continues, leaving all this to one side, straight to Los Cristianos, what was once a small fishing village how transformed into a point of bustling attraction with first class hotels and an important port. In its bay, together with the fishing fleet, there lie nearly all the important pleasure boats that exist in the island. A passenger ship regularly leaves Los Cristianos for the short journey to La Gomera.

It should be mentioned, however, that before reaching the end of the motorway in Los Cristianos, from which various good roads lead,

Güímar, in the valley of that name.

View of the South coast from the belvedere of La Centinela, in the Arona district.

The Coast of Silence.

off, we may find splendid places like the previously mentioned Coast of Silence, next to the little picturesque seaside village of Las Galletas, where there is a great tourist centre run by companies that are mixed Spanish and foreign or completely Tinerfeño. The Coast of Silence is a great place for those who want to forget the drudgery of the big cities, to find tranquillity and peace and to be in full contact with sun and sea. Without altering the peace and the silence that has given the district its name, there are strategically placed recreation centres which offer what is necessary for those who want to enjoy themselves in other ways.

Before the Coast of Silence we come to one of the biggest beaches in Tenerife, the Médano, with more than three kilometres of light sand. Here too the original village of fishermen and peasants has turned into hotels and summer villas.

XII

THE CONFINES OF THE ISLAND

From Los Cristianos a wide, well cared for road goes along the shares of the island of Tenerife. As it advances we notice how the scenery becomes sweeter and the harsh, dry South is making way for darker lands with more vegetation and the air gets cooler. It is the west coast, which little by little reaches a point at which everything is different.

Adeja, an important place which is the centre of its district and the starting point for visits to it, contains historical memories. Its «Casa Fuerte», the mansion and stronghold of the former lord of the zone, recalls pirates' deeds, cannon shot, returns from expeditions and unloading of recaptured booty. On its coast, several beaches succeed one another such as ««El Bobo», La Caleta, Las Puntillas, El Cangrejo, «El Inglés»; they are barely separated by coves and small headlands. Another tourist complex has grown up here, with the resounding name of «Playa de las Américas»; there are five-star hotels, restaurants and shops. Following the road uphill we come to Guia de Isora, which is neither north nor south as they say in the island, with its outlets to the sea in the fishing and pleasure beaches of Alcalá, San Juan and Puerto de Santiago. There follow villages with names as strange to foreign ears as Chio, Chirche, Chiguergue, Arguayo and Tamaimo, half way between the mountain and the sea. The road forks, with one branch going to Santiago del Teide, a high agricultural locality

Another aspect of the Coast of Silence.

The Médano beach is one of the biggest and most beautiful in the island.

An aspect of Adeje.

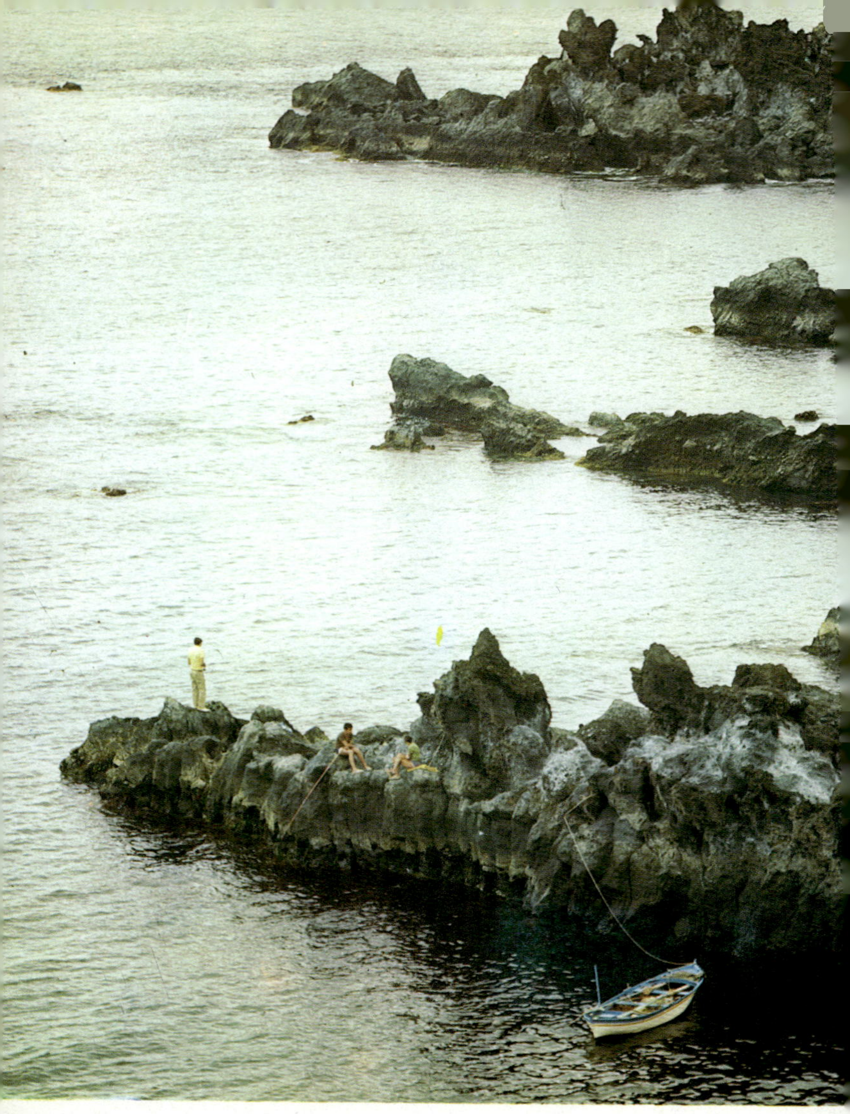

◀ As we proceed farther North, the West coast is becoming more rugged...

Church of St. James of the Teide.

Farther North, on the West coast, the little port of Alcalá.

with good soil and temperate and cold climate crops, a source of supply for the «creators of lands» who take the black soil to distant places where it may fulfil its mission of producing flowers and fruit. The other branch-road takes us to the most westerly point in the island, Teno, with a sheltered, almost virgin beach. Near it, amid splendid scenery, is Acantilado de los Gigantes ('Giants' Cliff), which drops down almost sheer to the ocean. This zone has been used fot the erection of new complexes of hotels and residences.

We have virtually gone round the island, we have visited its interior, and going on from the «Land of Wheat» we can join up with the roads to the North that lead to Icod and thence to the capital, passing through villages of pure peasant atmosphere such as La Guancha and Icod el Alto.

XIII

LA PALMA, LA GOMERA AND EL HIERRO

These three islands, with Tenerife, form the province of Santa Cruz de Tenerife. They are considerably smaller; La Palma has an area of 728 square kilometres and about 80,000 inhabitants; La Gomera 378 km.^{2} and 30,000 inhabitants; El Hierro 270 km.^{2} and 7,000 inhabitants.

The smaller islands communicate with Tenerife by regular sea lines, and La Palma and El Hierro also maintain air communications.

It is said of La Palma that it is the «green island *par excellence* or the «pretty island»; it contains the greatest heights in the world in relation to its perimeter. In the centre of the island is the greatest crater known, that of the Caldera (Cauldron) de Taburiente, with a perimeter of 28 km., largeley covered with pine woods and 770 metres deep in places. It is an island of great beauty, to which the currents of water that rise between the Peñas make their contribution. Its singular attractiveness has led to its being declared a National Park. It is mountainous, and its highest point is the rock of the Muchachos, 2,423 m. above sea level.

The capital of the island is Santa Cruz de La Palma, where there are a sheltered and important harbour, a well stocked Natural History Museum, and fine 16th century buildings, St. Saviour's Church and the Town Hall. The fact that it is situated in a kind of half-submerged crater called La Caldereta gives the city a very curious appearance. Leaving the capital we come to Las Breñas, famous for tobacco and

....to culminate in the cliff of The Giants, on the Point of Teno.

other crops, with a tourist residence, a good hotel and other places to stay for the visitor.

Near the city is the Sanctuary of the Virgin of the Snows, Patron of the island, in whose honour large scale fiestas are held every five years.

Los Llanos de Ariadne is the second largest town in the island. This commercial and agricultural centre is a pleasant place, the more so because of the idiosyncrasy and friendliness of its people. Tazacorta, surrounded by banana-growing zones, has a small port and marvellous beaches; Puerto Naos, a small town with tourist activity and a nice beach of fine sand; Fuencaliente, the most southerly town in the island, surrounded by pines and vines; the volcanic zone, where «San Antonio» was recently in eruption, like «San Juan» years before, spread on this last occasion as the lava that poured into the sea formed a peninsula of several hectares, now converted into cultivated land by means of the usual difficult procedure of carting earth and spreading it on the stone; Maza, near which the cave of Belmaco contains interesting prehistoric carvings, not far from the island's airport; San Andrés y Sauce, with its forest of lindens and ferns, the leafiest in the archipelago, and Tijarafe, near which is the cave called «Cueva Bonita» into which the sea penetrates.

The island of La Gomera is rounded and mountainous; its capital, San Sebastián, is a picturesque place of more than 7,000 inhabitants. A most important historical memory is the Torre del Conde (the Count's Tower), in its time the fortress and residence of the counts of the island. This island, described as Colombian *par excellente*, contributed with seamen and victuals to the discovery of the New Continent. Another important place is Hermigua, with its white, shining houses surrounded by the richest banana plantations in the island. Vallehermoso is extraordinarily beautiful; around the urban centre grow several species of fruit trees, palms and bananas. It has a lovely beach, near which is the cliff called Los Organos because of its curious shape. Another important place is Playa de Santiago, inhabited chiefly by fishermen near whose homes is a pleasant beach with clear water, and lastly Valle Gran Rey, set in a rich zone of bananas that almost reach its beautiful beach of golden sand.

The Cedar Wood, one of the finest in the Canaries, surprises us by its nearness to dry zones which it suddenly interrupts to turn into a green, moist and leafy area.

El Hierro, the smallest of the seven «big islands», is perhaps the most rugged of them all. In its small area, triangular in shape with high cliffs, there is a high central plateau; its highest point, at Malpaso, is 1,320 metres above sea level.

Santa Cruz de La Palma. The Plaza de España with the renaissance Palace of the City Council.

Façade of The Saviour's Church (c. 16) and monument to Manuel Díaz, in Santa Cruz de La Palma.

La Caldera de Taburiente has some of the most impressive scenery ▶ in the Canary archipelago.

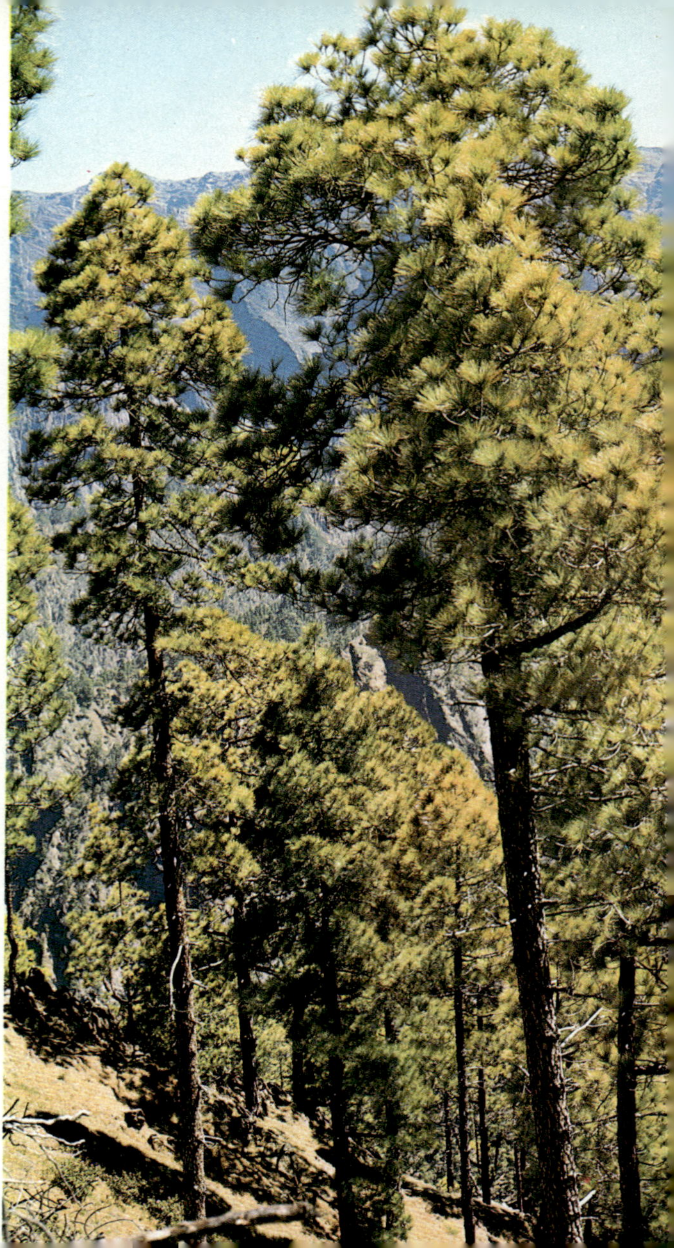

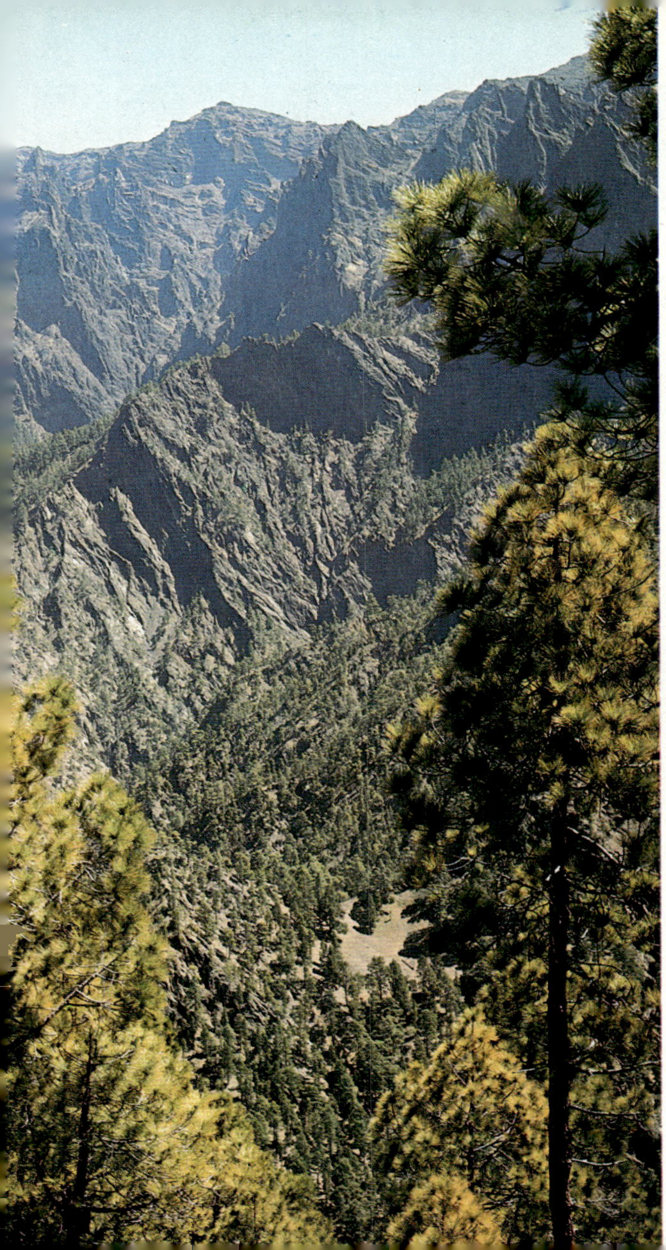

A peaceful corner of Los Llanos de Aridane, the second most important town in the island of La Palma.

Puerto Naos beach. ▶

The volcano of Teneguía, at the southern end of La Palma.

The Cave of Belmaco, with interesting drawings on the walls.

Los Sauces, surrounded by banana trees, in the North of the Island.

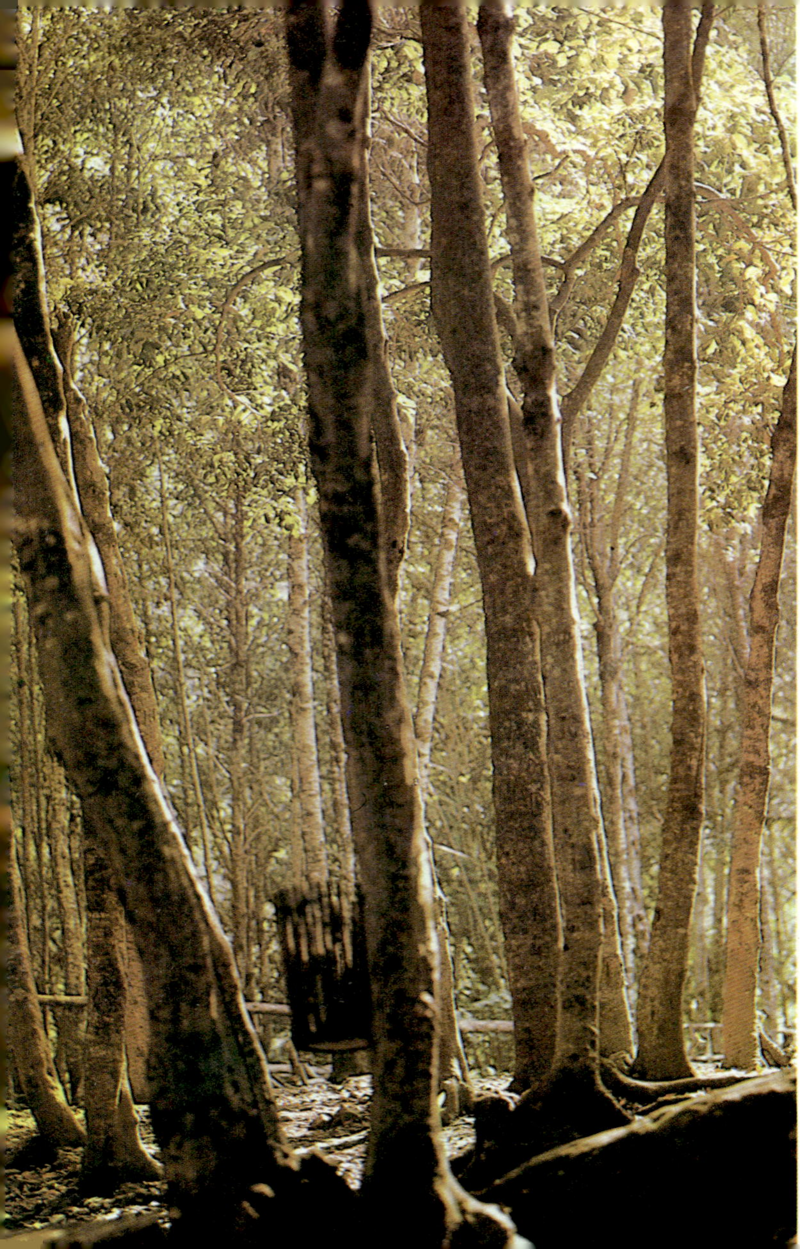

◀ Not far from Los Sauces, the impressive laurel woods of Los Tilos.

The Blue Pool at Puerto Espínola.

The coasts of El Hierro are cut almost sheer over the sea except for the district of El Golfo, 14 km. long and with wooded slopes that make it a beautiful place. The soil is verry fertile; the woods are chiefly composed of beeches and savins, some of which grow in old craters.

The capital is Valverde, with more than 4,000 inhabitants, an interesting town with a square that offers a pretty view of the sea. Some five kilometres away is the Puerto de La Estaca, which gives access to the island from the sea. Sabinosa, Frontera, El Monacal, Isora, Guarazoca and Los Taibiques are its urban centres.

Magnificent strong wine, delicious fruit, especially almonds, figs and «durazno» peaches, fine cheeses and the «quesadilla» which is the queen of the pastrycook's specialities in the Canaries, are products of El Hierro which are appreciated all over the archipelago. At Tamaduste a large natural swimming pool has attracted tourists and holiday-makers. The Salmor group of islets are worth a mention, where there are giant lizards which astonish naturalists. This example of exotic fauna is almost extinct, but a careful watch is kept over those still living to prevent the hunting instinct or simple caprice from destroying the few remaining examples of this strange saurian, or perhaps reptile.

XIV

CUSTOMS, FOLKLORE AND GASTRONOMY

As the Tinerfeño is the descendant of Spaniards, it is natural that his customs, amusements and folklore should be similar to those of his ancestors from the Peninsula. There is something in this, but there is also something, perhaps a great deal, that has been created thanks to isolation and remoteness. The old Guanches also left something before disappearing from the face of the planet, and, finally, something else has been left by those who emigrated to the Americas and returned to the their land. Thus a special form of living, of being and of relationships has been created. The manifestations are naturally easier to appreciate, so we shall give preference to them.

In the first place, the Tinerfeño is not fond of telling his problems to strangers. He prefers to talk only of his joys. He is a man of few words, maybe because of difficulties in expressing himself. Thus while the Andalusian is talkative, the Tinerfeño, and the Canary islander in general, is usually laconic. He respects other people's opinions, or at least does not warmly display his dissent. He prefers facts. The

At San Sebastián de la Gomera there rises the Count's Tower, a principal witness to the history of the island of Gomera.

Santiago beach, in the South of Gomera.

The Cano Rock, at Vallehermoso.

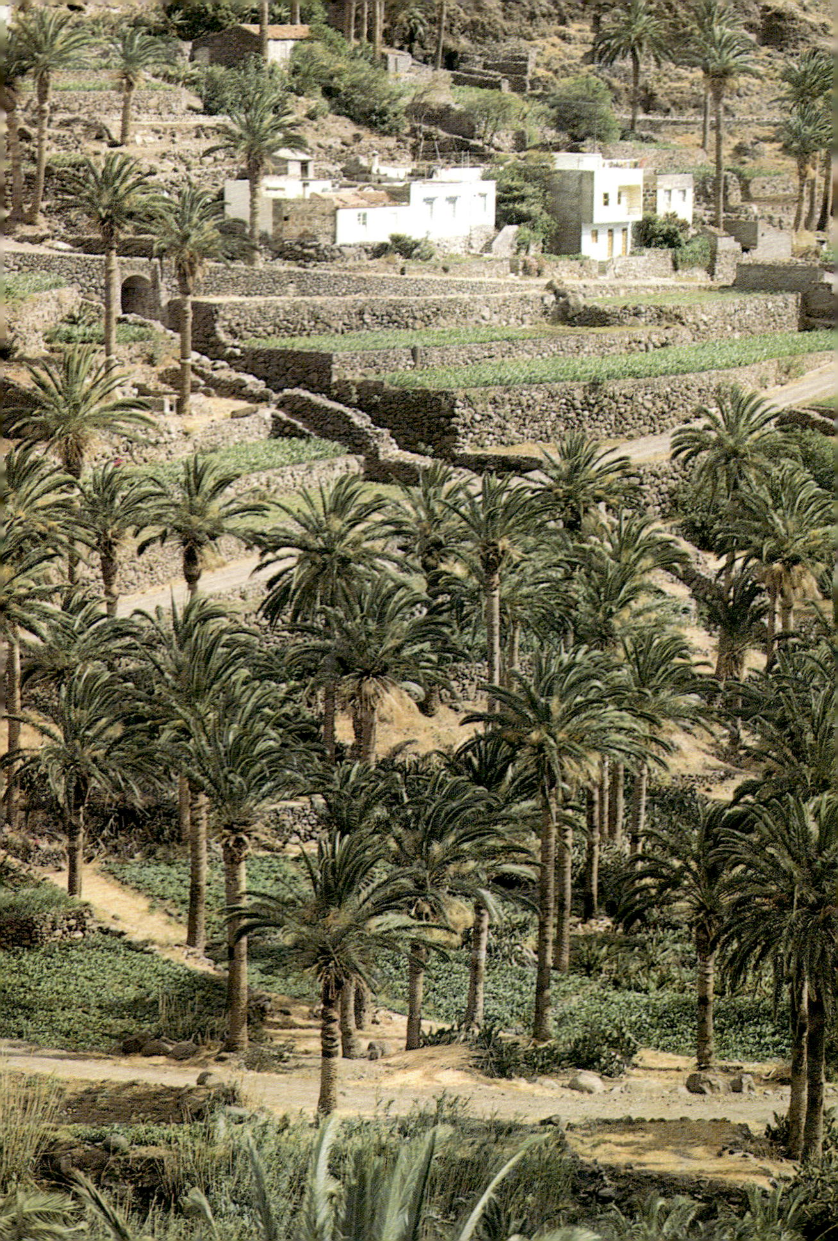

Gran Rey Valley is one of the strangest landscapes in the archipelago.

Beach at Gran Rey Valley.

Near Valverde, Tamaduste is the tourist capital of the island.

View of Valverde, capital of the island of Hierro.

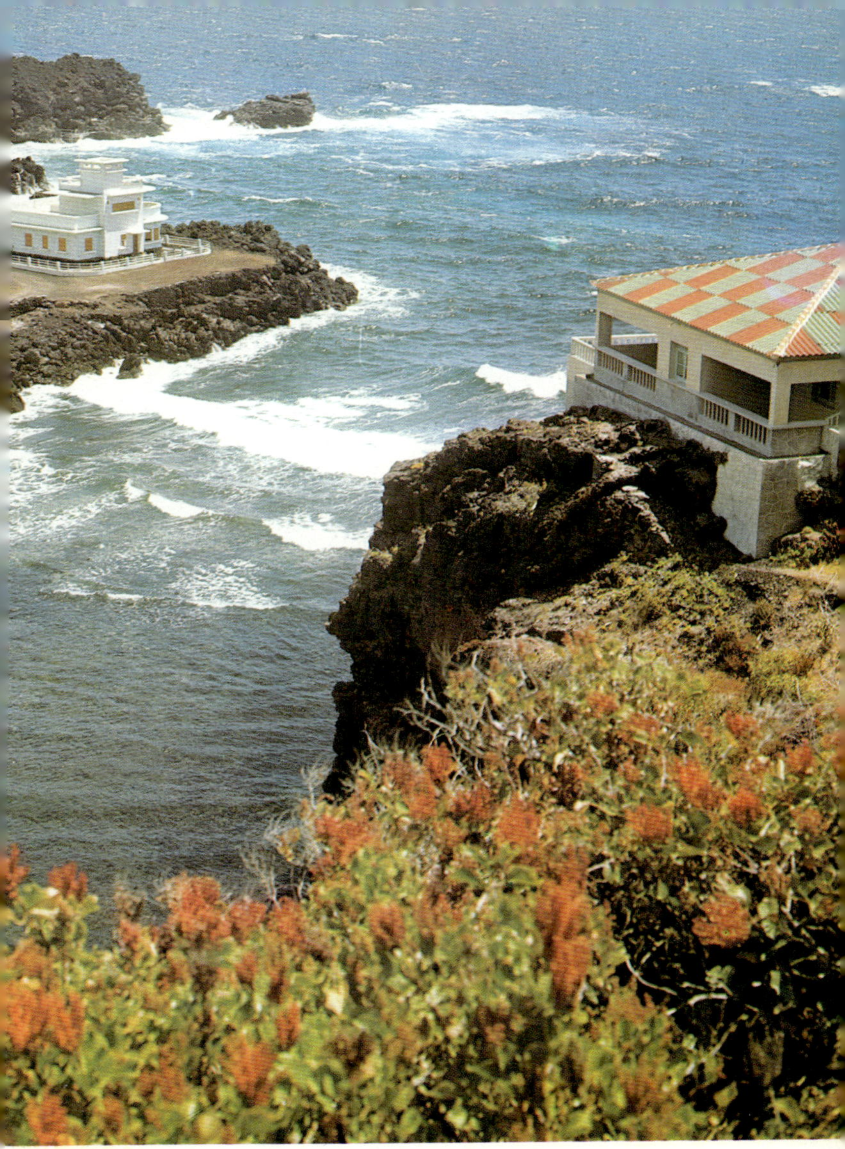

View of El Golfo, on the North shore of the island.

Frontera, chief town of the second municipality of the island of Hierro, nestles in the despression of El Golfo.

family is the important thing for him, but he considers as family his parents, his wife and children, no one else. Those who live under his roof compose the family; the rest are only relations or distant relations, even if the ties of blood are fraternal.

The Tinerfeña woman, especially the peasant one, is not fond of leaving her home. She works, has her children, suffers or laughs and dies in it. Only when she is young and unmarried is she capable of having a relatively intense social life.

Next in the loves and preferences of the Canario and the Tinerfeño comes the land. For the Tinerfeño the «pedacito» or the «fisco», as he calls his property, is worthy of every labour and every sacrifice. Attached to his land, to his village and his country, the islander works in silence and, without bragging, has come to achieve or to complete great undertakings.

The island folk music sometimes recalls the «jota», though the «Isa» is slower; or the gentle songs of the Andalusian coast, such as the «malagueña», and certain songs of Portugal and Extremadura, of which the «folia» is especially sweet.

The are also the lively, roguish «tanganillo», the graceful «seguidilla», the agitated «ajarastes» and «saltonas» or the slower «Santo Domingo» with its flavour of old Spanish. The vigorous «canto del güeyero» seems to recall the airs of the Cantabrian, while there are also songs from other islands, such as the «polka».

Guitars and stringed instruments, especially the diminutive but sonorous «timple», are the favourites when there is some festivity and serve for the groups of «players» and «singers» that form the «parrandas» which pass through the scene of the celebration, while the wines of the country are eagerly drunk, accompanied by «papas arrugadas», the classical potatoes cooked in their skins in a strong saline solution dipped in strong sauces or «mojos», with the meat or fish, while the piquant, strong-smelling «mojos» burn their throats and their scents call from afar.

The island cuisine has not much variety, as is fitting for a sober people. However, its flavours more than make up for its comparative gastronomical poverty.

The «gofío», a flour obtained after toasting wheat, maize, barley or chickpeas, adding a pinch of salt, was for many years the basic food of the Canaries. Kneaded in a bag of tanned goatskin with a little water or milk, it served as the basis of the meal, after soaking it in «mojo» or rubbing it with the «condute», that is to say with a piece of meat, fish or cheese that gave it a stronger flavour.

The «papas arrugadas» are also an obligatory accompaniment for various dishes of both meat and fish. The fish is generally only boiled

Terraces for cultivation at Vilaflor. ▶

Canary pesasant in the threshing floor.

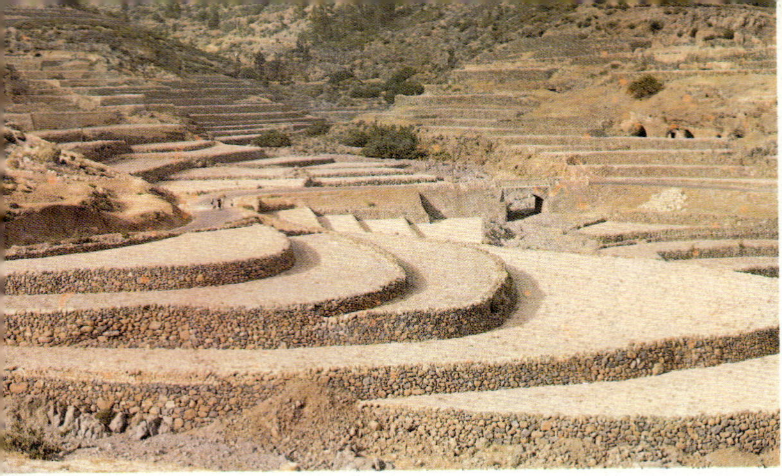

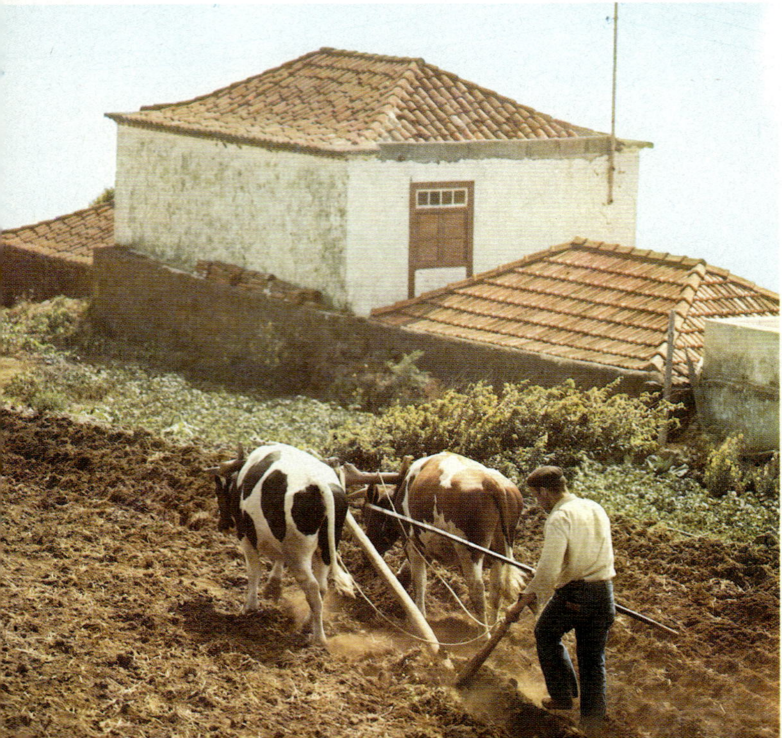

in water and salt; then «mojo» is poured on it and «papas» are served with it. If it is salted, the «mojo» must be stronger and more piquant.

The favourite meats are kid and rabbit, prepared in «salmorejo», a sauce with vinegar, garlic and herbs that gives an exquisite flavour and aroma. Pork, in pickle sauce with a penetrating smell that spreads far and awakes the appetite, is also a dish for fiestas.

The stew called «puchero», with meat, potatoes and vegetables, hardly ever without chickpeas, is very often to be found on the island table, and stewed dishes of pumpkin, such as «bubango», a specially tasty gourd, squashes or cabbage are frequently eaten. There are also delicious stews with fresh or salt fish, and some cereal soups. Lastly, the «tumbo», which is what is left in the pot and eaten next day, and «escalón», a strong winter dish of «gofio» kneaded with boiling water, pig's lard and seasoning, which is mixed with bacon, meat and vegetables.

Sweets are made on a base of honey or brown sugar, worked into puff pastry and easy to digest; while the «frangolo» is a kind of pudding made with roughly crushed maize, then boiled with milk and cinnamon, which when cold hardens and is covered with honey of cane or sugar.

The picture, short in fact but very pleasant tasting, is completed with the more consistent and coveted almond cakes.

In the island of La Palma, some loaves of sugar, honey, «gofio» and almonds, in varying proportions, are called «rapaduras». In this island they also make a tasty «almond cheese», and in El Hierro the magnificent «quesadilla», both tasty and nourishing, on the basis of fresh cheese, ground almonds, yolk of egg aund sugar, which only the people of the small island know how to prepare and bake perfectly.

As liquors, the people in the fields drink «mistela», a combination of strong coffee, sugar and «aguardiente» or «caña», which can also be made from grapes. The people of the sea prefer, besides the rum they have always enjoyed, «yerbita», which is nothing but either of the two aguardientes available, with an infusión of fragrant crushed herbs.

A good and sought-after dish is the tasty «vieja», a white fish of exquisite texture and taste, which must be eaten hot when it has just come out of the pot in which it has been boiled for a few minutes in water, preferably sea-water. It is served with a little oil and vinegar mixed with a couple of spoonfuls of water from the pot, though many enthusiasts add to this slight sauce a tremendously strong green or red pepper which receives very disrespectful names. The «vieja» is always accompanied by «papas arrugasas», by the «black» and «pretty» varieties when possible.

On teast days the villager and the peasant amuse themselves by singing, eating and drinking, though sometimes they also decide to

Ploughing the *malpaises* in the island of La Palma.

Popular pilgrimage dance.

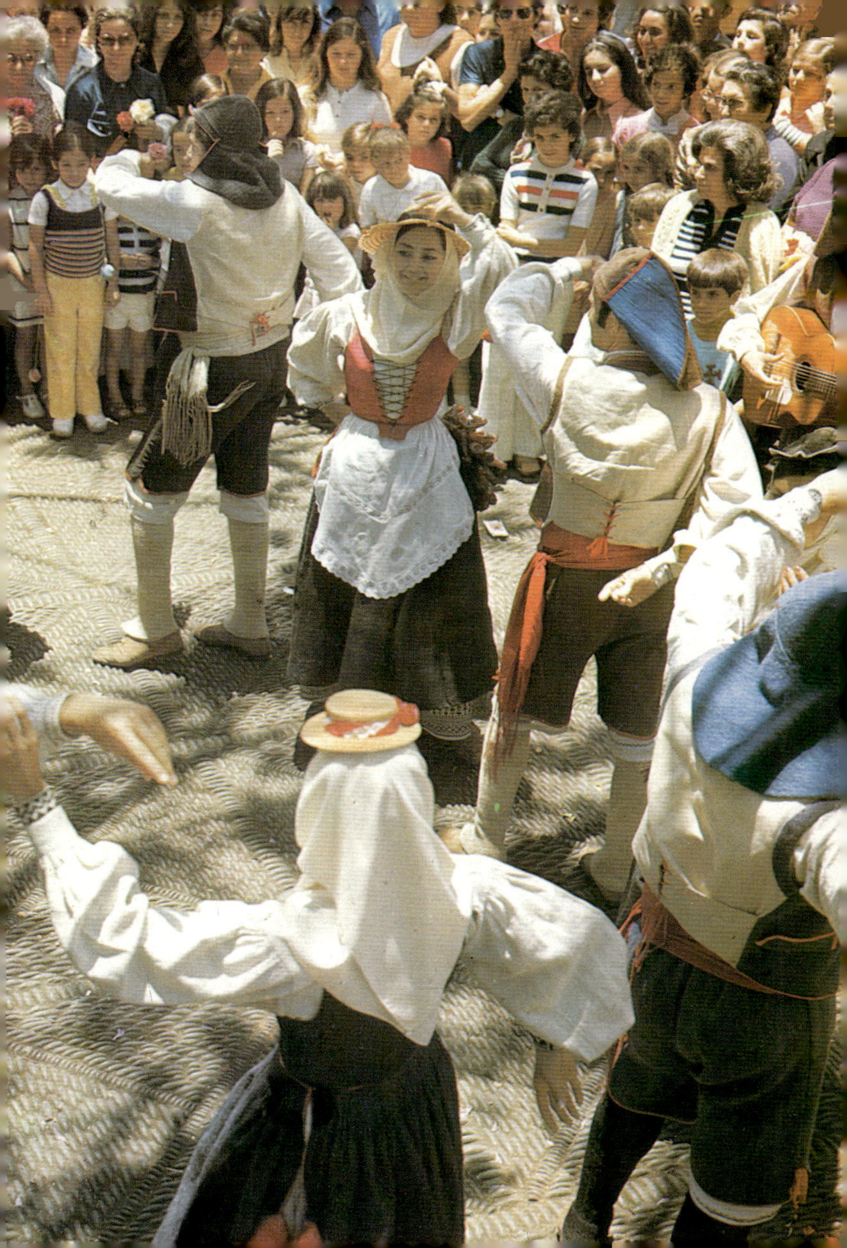

dance some «saltonas» or «seguidillas» or an «isa». The fiesta is generally based on a religious celebration, and there are two especially important occasions. These are the annual pilgrimages held in La Laguna and La Orotava in honour of St. Benedict and St. Isidore respectively. These pilgrimages are a complete expression of local customs and make an admirable spectacle. Thousands of pilgrims of both sexes, dressed in the old peasant costumes, dance and sing, ride in decorated carts or on horseback or on mules as they accompany the saint in procession. Groups sing the airs of the land in perfect harmony. The glossy cattle, prepared for the occasion, form part of the procession.

After the fiesta everbody returns to peace. The man and woman who had sung and danced recover their serious mien, and go back to their work in silence, eagerly. And it is thus, only thus, that it has been possible to make the islands the miracle represent.

XV

INTERNAL AND INTER-ISLAND COMMUNICATION

There are no railways in the Canaries, so that all land communications are made by road.

In the case of Tenerife, wide roads run all round the island. Two motorways start from the capital. One goes to Puerto de la Cruz, and it is planned to extend it as far as Icod de Los Vinos; it will then continue as a general road and end at Buenavista del Norte. The other, going through the South to Los Cristianos, joins a new road going up the west coast until it runs into the general north road and thus completes the circuit. There are also State and provincial auxiliary roads making contact with every locality in the island; while a road runs along the central spine of the island, from La Esperanza to Granadilla de Abona.

The island of La Palma has roads that leave the capital in two directions: to the north, as far as Barlovento, and to the south as far as Garafía; this latter road is prolonged on the western side and then goes north also. Another road crosses the island from east to west, from Santa Cruz de La Palma to Los Llanos de Ariadne.

In La Gomera a road runs west from San Sebastián; half way along its course it forks, with one branch going to Arure and Vallehermoso and the other to Agulo; these two localities are connected by a secondary road, and there are branch roads to Playa de Santiago, Alajeró and Calera.

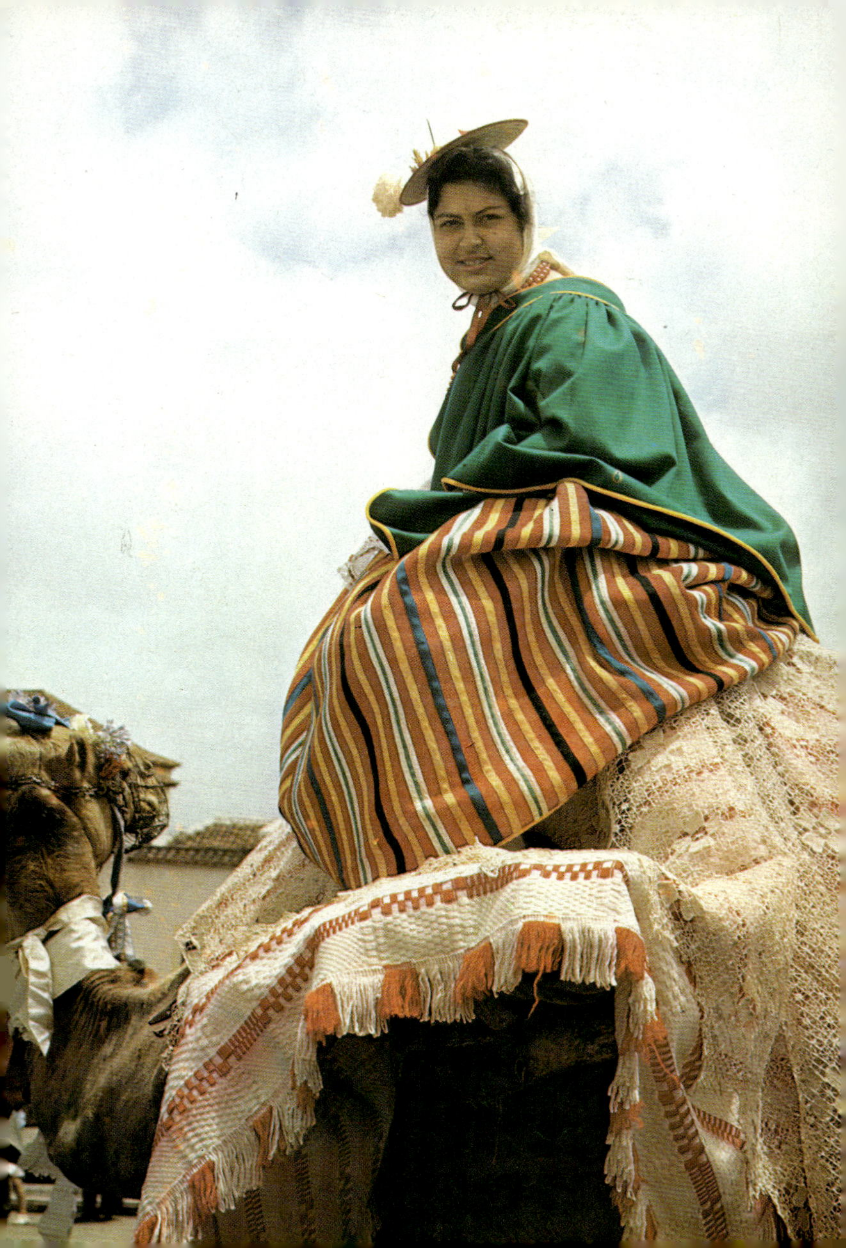

◀ Girl dressed in the typical costume in the pilgrimage of St. Isidore, in La Orotava.

The pilgrimage of St. Isidore, patron of La Orotava, is a folk festival full of colour and gaiety.

Pilgrimage to the sanctuary of Our Lady of the Snows, patron of La Palma.

El Hierro has motor roads leaving Valderde; a road to the latter has been built from Puerto de la Estaca, so one can virtually drive round the island.

With regard to sea communications, the port of Santa Cruz de Tenerife is conected by regular lines with Spain and almost all Europe. There are weekly services to Cádiz, Málaga, Barcelona, Valencia, Alicante, and the Cantabrian and Atlantic ports. There are also direct services to London and other British ports and to the coast towns of the European Atlantic and Mediterranean countries. It is also a port of call for the regular lines sailing the American, South African and Indian Ocean routes.

In the air there are several regular daily services to Madrid, Seville and Barcelona, and the islands are connected with one another by regular flights, several times a day with the neighbouring province of Las Palmas and to La Palma and El Hierro.

Several flights leave daily for París, Hamburg, Vienna, Stockholm and Brussels among other capitals, plus numerous charter flights, about fifty of them, which complete the daily movement of the Tenerife airport.

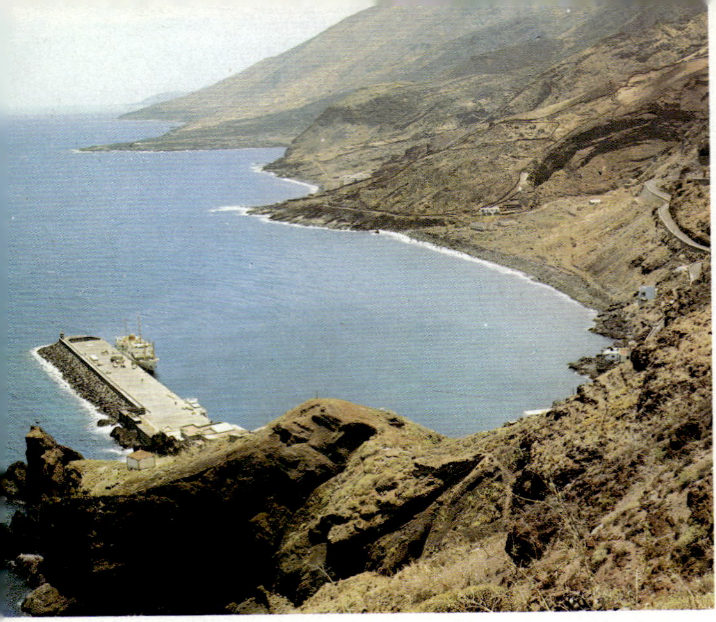

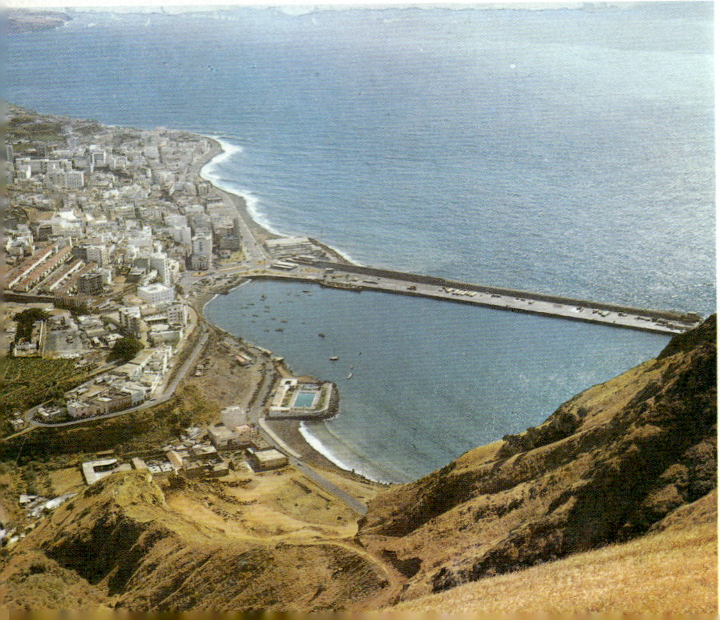

◀ Puerto de la Estaca, in the island of Hierro.

The harbour of Santa Cruz de Tenerife.

◀ General view of Santa Cruz de la Palma, with its ample roadstead.

Roads in the Canaries follow a difficult route at times, like this one crossing the ravine of El Time, in the island of La Palma.

Canary Island Romery.

INFORMACION PRACTICA TENERIFE
INFORMATION PRATIQUE TENERIFE
PRACTICAL INFORMATION TENERIFE
PRAKTISCHE HINWELSE TENERIFE

Para cualquier otra información, puede usted dirigirse a la Oficina de Turismo de esta localidad, sita en: Avda. José Antonio (Palacio Insular).

Pour toute information, vous pouvez vous adresser au Bureau du Turisme de cette ville, situé: Av. José Antonio (Palais Insulaire).

For further information, visit the Tourist Office in this town, located at: Av. José Antonio (Insular Palace).

Zur Erhaltung irgendeiner anderen Auskunft können Sie sich an das Turismusbüro dieser Ortschaft in der Av. José Antonio (Insularpalast).

ARCHIPIELAGO CANARIO
ARCHIPEL DES CANARIES
THE CANARIES ARCHIPELAGO
DER KANARISCHE ARCHIPEL

Tenerife, Gran Canaria, La Palma, La Gomera, El Hierro, Fuerteventura y Lanzarote, con los islotes de Islas de Lobos, Alegranza, Graciosa, Roque del Este y Roque del Oeste.
Está dividido en dos provincias: Tenerife, La Palma, La Gomera y El Hierro, con SANTA CRUZ DE TENERIFE como capital.
Y Gran Canaria, Fuerteventura, Lanzarote e islotes, con LAS PALMAS DE GRAN CANARIA como capital.

Posición geográfica:

27° 44'-29° 15' latitud N. y 13° 26'-17° 53' longitud W.

Altura máxima del Archipiélago.

Pico del Teide, 3.716 m.
Extensión superficial: 7.543 km. cuadrados.
Extensión de la provincia de Santa Cruz de Tenerife: 3.444 km. cuadrados.
Extensión de la isla de Tenerife: 2.058 km²
Habitantes en la isla de Tenerife: 560.000.
Distancias en millas desde el puerto de Santa Cruz de Tenerife a los de las otras islas y costas de Africa:

A las Palmas de Gran Canaria	54
A Santa Cruz de La Palma	102
A Arrecife (Lanzarote)	186
A San Sebastián de La Gomera	153
A Puerto del Rosario (Fuert.)	156
A Valverde (El Hierro)	156
A Cabo Juby (Costa de Africa)	180

Tenerife es un triángulo cuyos vértices son:
Punta de Anaga (vértice NE), Punta de Teno (vértice NW) y Punta de la Rasca (vértice S).
Lado mayor: Anaga-Teno, 80 km.
Lado menor: Rasca-Teno, 45 km.

Ténérife, Grande Canarie, La Palma, La Gomera, El Hierro, Fuerteventura et Lanzarote avec les îlots de Islas de Lobos, Alegranza, Graciosa, Roque del Este et Roque del Oeste. Il est divisé en deux provinces: Tenerife, La Palma, La Gomera et El Hierro avec SANTA CRUZ DE TENERIFE comme capitale.
Et La Grande Canarie, Fuerteventura, Lanzarote et les îlots avex LAS PALMAS DE GRAN CANARIA comme capitale.

Position géographique:

27° 44'-29° 15' latitude Nord et 13° 26'-17° 53' longitude Ouest.

Altitude maximum de l'archipel:

Pic du Teide, 3716 mètres.
Extension: 7543 km²
Extension de la province de Santa Cruz de Ténérife: 3444 km².
Extension de l'île de Ténérife: 2058 km².
Habitants de l'île de Ténérife: 560000.
Distances en milliers de km entre le port de Santa Cruz de Tenerife et ceux des autres îles et côtes d'Afrique:

A Las Palmas de Gran Canaria	54
A Santa Cruz de La Palma	102
A Arrecife (Lanzarote)	186
A San Sebastián de La Gomera	153
A Puerto del Rosario (Fuertev.)	156
A Valverde (El Hierro)	156
A Cabo Juby (Côte d'Afrique)	180

Ténérife a la forme d'un triangle dont les sommets sont:
Punta de Anaga (sommet NE) Punta de Teno (NO) Punta de la Rasca (Sud).
Plus grand côté: Anaga-Teno 80 km.
Plus petit côté: Rasca-Teno 45 km.

It consists of Tenerife, Gran Canaria, La Palma, La Gomera, El Hierro, Fuerteventura and Lanzarote together with the small islands Islas de Lobos, Alegranza, Graciosa, Roque del Este and Roque del Oeste.
It is divided into two provinces: Tenerife, La Palma, La Gomera and El Hierro, whose capital is SANTA CRUZ DE TENERIFE, and Gran Canaria, Fuerteventura, Lanzarote and the small islands, whose capital is LAS PALMAS DE GRAN CANARIA.

Geographical Position

27° 44'-29° 15' Latitude N. and 13° 26'-17° 53' Longitude W.

Highest point of the Archipelago:

Pico del Teide, 3,716 metres.
Surface area: 7,543 sq. kilometres.
Surface area of the province of Santa Cruz de Tenerife: 3,444 sq. km.
Surface area of Tenerife Island: 2,058 sq. km.
Population of Tenerife Island: 560.000.
Some distances from the port of Santa Cruz de Tenerife (in miles):

Las Palmas de Gran Canaria	54
Santa Cruz de La Palma	102
Arrecife (Lanzarote)	186
San Sebastián de La Gomera	153
Puerto del Rosario (Fuertv.)	156
Valverde (El Hierro)	156
Cabo Juby (African Coast)	180

Tenerife is a triangle whose vertices are Anaga Point (North-east), Teno Point (North-west), and Rasca Point (South).
Longest side: Anaga-Teno, 80 km.
Shortest side: Rasca-Teno, 45 km.

Der kanarische Archipel besteht aus folgenden Inseln: Teneriffa, Gran Canaria, La Palma, La Gomera, El Hierro, Fuerteventura und Lanzarote mit den kleinen Inseln Islas de Lobos, Alegranza, Graciosa, Roque del Este und Roque del Oeste.

Dei Inselgruppe gliedert sich in zwei Provinzen: Tenerife, La Palma, La Gomera und El Hierro mit SANTA CRUZ DE TENERIFE als Hauptstadt, Gran Canaria, Fuerteventura, Lanzarote und kleine Inseln mit LAS PALMAS DE GRAN CANARIA als Hauptstadts.

Geographische Lage:

27° 44'-29° 15' Breitengrand N und 13° 26'-17° 53' Längengrand W.

Hochstpunkt des Archipels:

Pico del Teide 3.716 m.
Oberfläche: 7.543 qkm.
Oberfläche der Provinz von Santa Cruz de Tenerife: 3.444 qkm.
Oberfläche der Insein Teneriffa: 2.058 qkm.
Einwohnerzahl der Inseln Teneriffa: 560.000.
Entfernungen in Meilen vom Hafen Santa Cruz de Tenerife zu den Häfen der anderen Inseln und Küsten Afrikas:

Nach Las Palmas de Gran Canaria	54
Nach Santa Cruz de La Palma	102
Nach Arrecife (Lanzarote)	186
Nach San Sebastián auf La Gomera	153
Nach Puerto del Rosario (Fuerteventura)	156
Nach Valverde (El Hierro)	156
Nach Kap Juby (Küste Afrikas)	180

Teneriffa is ein Dreieck, dessen Ekken folgande Landzungen bilden: Punta de Anaga (NO-Ecke). Punta de Teno (NW-Ecke) und Punta de la Rasca (S-Ecke).
Längste Seite: Anaga-Teno 80 km.
Kürzeste Seite: Rasca-Teno 45 km.

COSTAS DE TENERIFE
COTES DE TENERIFE
THE COASTLINE OF TENERIFE
DIE KÜSTEN TENERIFFAS

La costa norte de Tenerife es alta y acantilada; en cambio, la del sur presenta zonas más bajas, en las que alternan las playas con el roquedo. La costa de Anaga es acantilada, excepto en la desembocadura de los barrancos. A partir de Punta Hidalgo, donde termina la zona de Anaga, la costa se hace más baja, pero sin dejar de ser acantilada, para volver a elevarse y mantenerse por encima de los 100 metros, en casi todo su trayecto hasta el valle de La Orotava. El tramo correspondiente al valle de La Orotava forma en casi todo su recorrido un acantilado de unos 70 metros, excepto donde se asienta el Puerto de la Cruz. El tramo norte restante sigue siendo escarpado hasta la zona de Teno, en que la línea contigua del acantilado queda un poco alejada del actual litoral. El Sur de Teno posee los mayores acantilados de la isla. La costa de la comarca sur es más baja, con algunas playas y pequeños puertos, como Los Cristianos y El Médano. La costa del valle de Güimar, muy rocosa, es más baja que las de las zonas próximas.

La côte nord de Ténérife est haute et formée de falaises; par contre celle du sud présente des zones plus basses où alternent les plages et les falaises. La côte de Anaga est aussi formée falaises sauf l'embouchure des ravins. A partir de Punta Hidalgo où se termine la zone de Anaga la côte devient plus basse mais sans perdre ses falaises, pour s'élever à nouveau et se maintenir au-dessus des 100 mètres dans presque tout son trajet jusqu'à la Vallée de La Orotava. Le tronçon correspondant à La Orotava forme presque tout son parcours une falaise d'environ 70 metres sauf à l'endroit du Puerto de la Cruz. Le tronçon nord demeure escarpé jusqu'à la zone de Teno où la ligne continue de la falaise reste un peu en retrait du littoral actuel. Le Sud de Teno possède les plus grandes falaises de l'île. La côte de la région sud est la plus basse, avec quelques plages et petits ports comme Los Cristianos et El Médano. La côte de la vallée de Güimar, très rocheuse, est plus basse que celles des zones proches.

Along the north coast of Tenerife there are high cliffs, whilst the southern part of the island is lower, sandy beaches alternating with rocks. The coastline of Anaga is steep, except at the mouths of the gorges. After Punta Hidalgo, where the Anaga district ends, there are lower cliffs, but it then rises again to heights over 100 metres, this formation continuing as far as La Orotava Valley; the stretch corresponding to La Orotava valley is some 70 metres high with the exception of the area where Puerto de la Cruz lies. The remaining northerly stretch continues steep as far as the Teno district, where the line of cliffs lies back from the actual seashore; towards the south of Teno, you can see the best cliffs on the island. The southern coastline is lower with several beaches and little ports such as Los Cristianos and El Médano. The shores of the Valley of Güimar are very low and rocky.

Die Nordküste ist hoch und fällt steil ab. Dagegen sind an der Südküste niedrigere Zonen, in denen sich Strände und Felsen abwechseln, zu verzeichnen. Die Küste von Anaga ist schroff und steil abfallend; eine Ausname bildet die Mündung der Schluchten. Von der Punto (Landzunge) de Hidalgo an, wo das Gebiet. Von Anaga aufhört wird die Küste flacher, ist aber weiterhin steil. Sie steigt dann wieder etwas an und hält sich auf fast der ganzen Strecke bis zum Tal von La Orotava in einer Höhe von über 100 m. Der dem Tal von La Orotava entsprechende Abschnitt ist fast ausschliesslich 70 m. hohe Steilküste, ausgenommen der Landstrich von Puerto de la Cruz. Der übrige nördliche Teil bleibt weiterhin steil und abschüssig bis zum Gebietsstreifen von Teno. Hier entfernen sich die steilen Klippen ein wenig von der gegenwärtigen Kustenlinie. Der Süden von Teno besitz die höchste Steilküste. Die Küste des südlichen Landstriches ist flacher; hier tauchen hin und wieder Strände und kleine Häfen auf, wie z.B. Los Cristianos und El Médano. Die felsige Küste des Tales von Güimar ist niedriger als die der umlegenden Gebiet.

ARTE Y CULTURA
ART ET CULTURE
ART AND CULTURE
KUNST UND KULTUR

.1. CONJUNTO MONUMENTAL
ENSEMBLE MONUMENTAL
MONUMENTS
SEHENSWÜRDIGKEITEN

anta Cruz de Tenerife

CASTILLO DE PASO ALTO.
CHATEAU DE PASO ALTO.
ASO ALTO CASTLE.
URG PASO ALTO.

Monumento a los héroes del 25 de mayo de 1797 (victoria sobre el almirante Nelson). Puede verse en este museo militar el cañón «Tigre», una de cuyas balas arrancó el brazo del almirante inglés.

Monument aux héros du 25 mai 1797 (victoire sur l'Amiral Nelson). Dans ce musée militaire on peut voir le canon «Tigre», l'une des balles duquel arracha le bras de l'amiral anglais.

Monument to the heroes of 25th May 1797 (victory over Admiral Nelson). In the military museum, visitors can see the cannon «Tigre», one of the balls from which took off the English Admiral's arm.

In Denkmal für die Helden des 25. Mai 1797 (Sieg über den Admiral Nelson). In diesen Militärmuseum ist die Kanone «Tiger» zu sehen, von deren Kugeln eine den Arm des englischen Generals abriss.

IGLESIA DE LA CONCEPCION.
EGLISE DE LA CONCEPTION.
CHURCH OF LA CONCEPCION.
KIRCHE «LA CONCEPCION».

Construida en el siglo XVI y reconstruida después de un incendio en el XVII, es el templo más importante, en cuyas cinco naves se guardan interesantes muestras del estilo barroco y los más valiosos recuerdos históricos de las Canarias. Aquí se conserva la Cruz de la Conquista y las banderas arrebatadas al almirante Nelson, con motivo de su frustrado ataque a la plaza. La Capilla de Carta, prodigio de talla en madera a mano, y la hermosa sillería de coro, hoy instalada en el presbiterio, son también de interés artístico.

Construite au 16ᵉ s. et reconstruite après un incendie au 17ᵉ, c'est le temple le plus important. Dans ses cinq nefs on montre d'intéressantes traces du style baroque et des souvenirs historiques de la plus grande valeur des îles Canaries. On conserve ici la Croix de la Conquête et les drapeaux arrachés à l'amiral Nelson, lors de son attaque frustré à la place. La Capilla de Carta, chef-d'oeuvre de sculpture de bois à la main, et la belle stalle du choeur, installée aujourd'hui au presbitérium, sont également d'intérêt artistique.

Built in the 16th century and rebuilt after a fire in the 17th, it is the biggest church and in its aisles can be found some interesting examples of the Baroque style and some valuable historical relics of the past of the Canary Islands. Here, the Cross of the Conquest is preserved, as well as the colours taken from Admiral Nelson during his unsuccessful attack on the fortress. The Carta Chapel, which is a Magnificent example of woodcarving, and the beautiful choir stalls are also of artistic interest.

Erbaut im 16. Jahrhundert und rekonstruiert nach einem Brand im 17. Jahrhundert, ist sie die bedeutendste Kirche, in deren fünf Schiffen interessante Zeugnisse des Barockstils und die wertvollsten historischen Erinnerungen der Kanarischen Inseln aufbewahrt werden. Hier befinden sich das Kreuz der Eroberung und die dem Admiral Nelson bei seinem vergeblichen Angriff auf den Platz abgenommenen Fahnen. Die Carta-Kapelle, eine wundervolle Handschnitzerei, und das prächtige Chorgestühl, das heute im Altarraum steht, sind ebenfalls von künstlerischem Interesse

IGLESIA DE SAN FRANCISCO.
EGLISE DE SAN FRANCISCO.
THE CHURCH OF SAN FRANCISCO.
KIRCHE DES HEILIGEN FRANZISKUS.

Portada barroca del siglo XVIII con columnas salomónicas. Son notables las imágenes de San Pedro de Alcántara, del mismo siglo, y el Señor de las Tribulaciones.

Son frontispice est baroque du 18ᵉ s. avec des colonnes salomon. Les images de Saint Pierre d'Alcántara, du même siècle, et le Seigneur des Tribulations, sont remarquables.

18th century Baroque façade with spiral columns. Also noteworthy are the images of Saint Peter of Alcántara, from the same century, and of the Christ of Tribulations.

Barockportal aus dem 18. Jahrhundert mit Salomonsäulen. Beachtlich sind die Bilder des Heiligen Petrus von Alcántara aus demselben Jahrhundert und des Hern der Drangsal.

MONUMENTO A LOS CAIDOS.
MONUMENT AUX MORTS.
MEMORIAL TO THE FALLEN.
GEFALLENENDENKMAL.

Artístico monumento con esbelta torre, provisto de ascensor que lleva a la parte alta.

C'est un artistique monument avec une tour élancée, munie d'un ascenseur qui conduit au sommet.

An artistic monument with a slender tower, equipped with a lift to take visitors to the top.

Artistisches Denkmal mit schlankem Turm, mit einem Aufzug, der in den oberen Teil führt.

MONUMENTO A LA CANDELARIA.
MONUMENT A LA CANDELARIA.
MONUMENT TO OUR LADY OF LA CANDELARIA.
DENKMAL DER MARIA REINIGUNG.

Simboliza la Adoración de la Virgen, Patrona del Archipiélago, por los guanches, primitivos pobladores. Este monumento fue construido en mármol de Carrara en 1718 y es debido al famoso escultor Casanova.

Symbolise la vénération des habitants primitifs, les guanches, pour la Vierge, patronne de l'Archipel. Le monument fut construit en 1718, en marbre de Carrare, par le fameux sculpteur Casanova.

It symbolizes the Adoration of the Virgin Mary, Patron Saint of the Archipelago, by the Guanches, the original inhabitants of the islands. It was built of Carrara marble in 1718 and is attributed to the famous sculptor Cassanova.

Ein Symbol für die Anbetung der Jungfrau, de Schutzherrin der Inselgruppe, durch die Guanchen, die ursprünglichen Bewohner Dieses Denkmal wurde aus Carrara-Marmo 1718 errichtet und ist dem berühmten Bildhauer Casanova zu verdanken.

PALACIO DE CARTA. *PALAIS DE CARTA.*
PALACE OF CARTA. *PALAST VON CARTA.*

Siglo XVIII. Característica arquitectura canari mezclada con elementos mudéjares y flamencos.

XVIII siècle. Architecture canarienne caractéristique mêlée à des éléments mudéjars e flamands.

18th century. Characteristic Canary architectur mixed with Mudejar and Flemish elements.

XVIII. Jahrhundert. Charakteristische kanarisch Architektur durchsetzt mit mudejar und flaemischen Elementen.

PALACIO INSULAR.
PALAIS INSULAIRE.
THE ISLAND PALACE.
INSELPALAST.

Moderno edificio de majestuosa traza, dond pueden admirarse unas magníficas pintura de José Aguiar.

C'est un édifice moderne de prestance majestueuse et où l'on peut admirer de magnifique peintures de José Aguiar.

A modern building with majestic lines, wher visitors may admire the magnificent painting of Jose Aguiar.

Ein majestätisch angelegtes, modernes Ge bäude, wo grossartige Gemälde von Jos Aguiar bewundert werden können.

La Laguna

IGLESIA DE SAN FRANCISCO.
EGLISE DE SAN FRANCISCO.
THE CHURCH OF SAN FRANCISCO.
KIRCHE DES HEILIGEN FRANZISKUS.

Donde se venera con gran devoción el Santísim Cristo de la Laguna. Esta imagen es una tab esbozada en madera de bornio de fines del XV en tamaño natural, atribuido a un artista ane nimo de la escuela sevillana. La imagen fu traida a Tenerife por el Adelantado D. Alons Fernández de Lugo.

On y vénère avec grande dévotion le Christ de L Laguna. Cette image est une planche étuvé en bois de la fin du 16ᵉ s. et de taille humaine on l'attribue à un artiste anonyme de l'éco sévillane. L'image fut transportée à Ténéri par l'amiral Alonso Fernández de Lugo.

Where the Christ of La Laguna is venerated with great devotion. The life-sized image is of decorated wood and is attributed to an anonymous artist of the Seville School of the late 15th century. It was brought to Tenerife by Governor Alonso Fernández de Lugo.

Dort wird mit grosser Hingabe der Allerheiligste Christus der Laguna verehrt. Dieses Bild ist ein Holz gearbeitetes Tafelbild vom Ende des 15. Jahrhunderts in natürlicher Grösse, das einem anonymen Künstler der Schule von Sevilla zugeschrieben wird. Das Bild wurde von dem Gouverneur Alonso Fernández de Lugo nach Teneriffa gebracht.

CATEDRAL. *CATHEDRALE.*
CATHEDRAL. *KATHEDRALE.*

Edificio con esbeltez equilibrada y en justa proporción sus columnas, arcos y bóvedas. El ábside es muy hermoso; su presbiterio, construido sobre cuatro gradas de mármol, es de inconfundible aire neogótico. El coro, legado por el arzobispo Bencomo, es neoclásico, como el trazado de la fachada. Dentro de este coro hay un facístol y en él, un pequeño crucifijo de Domingo Estévez. También puede admirarse el espléndido órgano construido en Londres, en 1857. En la capilla de los Remedios hay un retablo barroco de principios del siglo XVIII.

C'est un édifice svelte et bien proportionné dans ses colonnes, ses arcs et ses voûtes. L'abside est très belle; le presbyterium, construit sur quatre marches de marbre, est d'un estyle néogothique. Le choeur, don de l'archevêque Bencomo, est néoclassique, de même que le frontispice. Dans le choeur il y a un lutrin dominé par un petit crucifix de Domingo Estévez. On peut y admirer également un orgue splendide, construit à Londres en 1857. Dans la chapelle des Remedios il existe un retable baroque du 18ᵉ s.

A building whose slenderness is balanced and whose columns, arches and vaults are in correct proportion. The apse is extremely beautiful, while its presbytery, built on top of four marble steps has an unmistakable neo-Gothic air about it. The choir, a legacy from Archbishop Bencomo, is neo-Classical, as is the layout of the façade. Within this choir, there is a lectern on which there is a small crucifix by Domingo Estévez. Visitors can also admire the splendid organ which was built in London in 1857. In the Los Remedios Chapel, there is a Baroque altarpiece from the early 18th century.

Ein Gebäude von ausgeglichener schlanker Form, dessen Säulen, Bögen und Gewölberichtig proportioniert sind. Die Apsis ist sehr schön; sein Altarraum, errichtet auf vier Marmorstufen, hat ein unverkennbar neugotisches Aussehen. Der Chor, ein Legat des Erzbischofs Bencomo, ist neuklassisch, wie die Fassade. In diesem Chor befindet sich ein Chorpult und darin ein kleines Kruzifix von Domingo Estévez. Ebenfalls ist die herrliche, 1857 in London gebaute Orgel zu bewundern. In der Remedios-Kapelle befindet sich ein barockes Altarbild vom Anfang des 18. Jahrhunderts.

PALACIO DEL CABILDO.
PALAIS DU CABILDO.
THE CABILDO PALACE.
PALAST DES STADTRATES.

Se comenzó a construir en 1542; en su puerta, de estilo plateresco en piedra rosa, triunfan las armas de Carlos V y del Regidor Alvárez de Sotomayor.

On commença sa construction en 1542; sur sa porte, de style plateresque en pierre rose, figurent les armes de Charles-Quint et de l'échevin Alvarez de Sotomayor.

This building was begun in 1542; on its door, in pink stone in the plateresque style, can be seen the coats-of-arms of Carlos V and Alderman Alvarez de Sotomayor.

1542 wurde mit seinem Bau begonnem; auf seinem Tor, in plateraskem Stil aus rosa Stein, heben sich die Wappen von Karl V. und dem Stadtrat Alvarez de Sotomayor ab.

LA CONCEPCION. *LA CONCEPCION.*
LA CONCEPCION. *LA CONCEPCION.*

Gótica con elementos mudéjares. Principios del siglo XVI. Varias reformas, la más importante del siglo XVIII. Coros y púlpitos barrocos, magníficos.

Gothique avec éléments mudéjars. Début du XVI siècle. Plusieurs réformes, la plus importante au XVIII siècle. Choeurs et chaires magnifiques.

Gothic with Mudejar elements. Beginning of the 16th century. Several reformations, the most important in the 18th century. Baroque choirs and pulpits magnificent.

Gotisch mit mudejar Elementen. Anfang des XVI. Jahrhundert Verschiedene Aenderungen, die Wichtigste im XVIII. Jahrhundert. Choere und Kanzeln barok, praechtig.

PALACIO DE LOS CONDES DE SALAZAR.
PALAIS DES COMTES DE SALAZAR.
PALACE OF THE COUNTS OF SALAZAR.
PALAST DER GRAFEN VON SALAZAR.

Construido en el siglo XVII, en él se compaginan la suntuosidad y la gracia dados los ricos artesonados de sus interiores. En la actualidad se encuentra instalado aquí el Obispo.

Construit au 17ᵉ s., réunit à la fois, la somptuosité et la grâce de sa riche voûte à caissons. Actuellement l'Evêque réside là.

Built in the 17th century, it combines magnificence and grace in its priceless coffered ceilings. At present it is the Bishop's Residence.

Erbaut im 17. Jahrhundert. In ihm verbindet sich Prunk und Grazie durch das Täfelwerk in seinem Inneren. Gegenwärtig ist es der Bischofssitz.

PALACIO DE LOS VILLANUEVA DEL PRADO.
PALAIS DES VILLANUEVA DEL PRADO.
THE VILLANUEVA DEL PRADO PALACE.
PALAST DER VILLANUEVA DEL PRADO.

Reedificado a mediados del siglo XVIII, pleno de lujo y elegancia, fue sede de una famosísima tertulia erudita —1760 a 1770— que marcó surcos intelectuales y cuyo director fue el famoso historiador don Joseph de Viera y Clavijo.

Reconstruit au milieu du 18ᵉ s. plein de luxe et d'élégance, il fut le siège d'une fort fameuse réunion d'érudits —1760-1770— qui laisse des traces durables et dont le directeur fut le fameux historien Joseph de Viera y Clavijo.

Rebuilt in the middle of the 18th century, it is both luxurious and elegant. Between 1760 and 1770, it was a famous meeting place for the learned minds of the period, who blazed new trails in thinking under the leadership of the renowned historian, Joseph de Viera y Clavijo.

Neuerbaut Mitte des 18. Jahrhunderts, voller Luxus und Eleganz, war er Sitz eines berühmten Stammtisches von Gelehrten —1760 bis 1770— der intellektuelle Spuren hinterliess und dessen Leiter der berühmte Geschichtsschreiber Joseph de Viera y Clavijo war.

Puerto de La Cruz

ACANTILADO MARTIAÑEZ.
ACANTILADO MARTIAÑEZ.
THE MARTIAÑEZ CLIFFS.
STEILKÜSTE MARTIAÑEZ.

Lugar donde moraban los antiguos guanches y desde donde se divisa todo el término municipal de Puerto de La Cruz.

Lieu où habitaient les anciens guanches et d'où l'on contemple toute la commune du Puerto de La Cruz.

These were inhabited by the ancient Guanche peoples and from it the whole of Puerto de La Cruz can be seen.

Wohnort der ehemaligen Guanchen, von wo aus der ganze Bezirk Puerto de La Cruz zu sehen ist.

CASTILLO DE SAN FELIPE.
CHATEAU DE SAN FELIPE.
SAN FELIPE CASTLE.
BURG SAN FELIPE.

Antiguo fuerte junto al mar.

Ancien fort face à la mer.

An old fort on the shore.

Ehemalige Burg am Meer.

IGLESIA DE NUESTRA SEÑORA DE LA PEÑA DE FRANCIA.
EGLISE DE NOTRE-DAME DE LA PEÑA DE FRANCIA.
CHURCH OF OUR LADY OF THE PEÑA DE FRANCIA.
KIRCHE «NUESTRA SEÑORA DE LA PEÑA DE FRANCIA».

Construida en 1603, aquí se veneran las imágenes de Cristo del Gran Poder y de la Virgen del Carmen, patronos de la población.

Construite en 1603, on y vénère les images du Christ del Gran Poder et de la Vierge del Carmen, patronne de la ville.

Built in 1603, the images of Christ the Almighty and Our Lady of Mount Carmel, patron saints of the town are venerated here.

Erbaut 1603. Hier werden die Bilder des Allmächtigen Christus und der Jungfrau des Carmen verehrt, der Schutzheiligen des Ortes.

Santa Cruz de La Palma

AYUNTAMIENTO. *MAIRIE.*
TOWN HALL. *RATHAUS.*

Construido en 1563, es estilo renacimiento italiano. Todos los elementos de la construcción y ornamentación exterior son curiosamente asimétricos, pero tan armoniosamente conjuntados, que es necesario fijar la atención en el detalle para reparar en la asimetría.

Construite en 1563 en style renaissance italienne. Tous les éléments de la construction et de l'ornementation extérieure sont curieusement assymétriques, mais assemblés de telle manière qu'il faut prêter attention au détail pour en remarquer l'assymétrie.

Built in 1563 in the Italian Renaissance style. All the outside constructional and decorative elements are curiously asymmetrical and yet they are so harmoniously combined that it is necessary to carry out a detailed examination to notice this asymmetry.

Erbaut 1563, in italienischen Renaissancestil. Alle äusseren Bau und Zierelemente sind seltsam asymmetrisch, jedoch so harmonisch verbunden, dass man seine Aufmerksamkeit auf Einzelheiten richten muss, um die Asymmetrie wahrzunehmen.

PARROQUIA DEL SALVADOR.
PAROISSE DU SAUVEUR.
THE PARISH CHURCH OF EL SALVADOR.
PFARRKIRCHE DES «SALVADOR».

Es una de las construcciones religiosas más armoniosas y elegantes del Archipiélago. El pórtico, de cantería labrada, es de estilo renacentista. El artesonado, mudéjar. El techo de la sacristía, gótico, único ejemplar en la isla.

C'est l'une des constructions religieuses les plus élégantes et harmonieuses de l'Archipel. Le portique, en pierre taillée, est de style renaissance. La voûte à caissons est mudéjar, et le plafond de la sacristie, gothique, est un exemple unique dans toute l'île.

This is one of the most harmonious and elegant religious buildings in the Archipelago. The portico of dressed stonework is in the Renaissance style, the coffered ceilings are Mudejar, while the ceiling of the sacristy is Gothic, the only example of this style on the island.

Sie ist eine der harmonischsten und elegantesten kirchlichen Bauten des Archipels. Das Portal aus behauenem Stein ist Renaissancestil, das Täfelwerk Mudejar stil, die Decke der Sakristei gotisch, das einzige Beispiel dafür auf der Insel.

CASTILLO DE SANTA CATALINA.
CHATEAU DE SANTA CATALINA.
SANTA CATALINA CASTLE.
BURG VON SANTA CATALINA.

Siglo XVI. Reconstruido el siglo XVII. Planta cuadrada con cuatro baluartes en ángulo.

XVI siècle. Reconstruit au XVII siècle. Plan carré avec quatre bastions dans les angles.

16th century. Reconstructed in the 17th century. Square plan with four angular bastions.

XVI. Jahrhundert. Wiederaufgebaut im XVII. Jahrhundert. Viereckiger Grundriss mit vier Basteien an den Ecken.

La Orotava

LA CONCEPCION.
LA CONCEPCION.
LA CONCEPCION.
LA CONCEPCION.

Siglo XVIII. Sigue el tipo de basílica florentina de Brunelleschi. Tabernáculo neoclásico.

XVIII siècle. Suit le type de basilique florentine de Brunelleschi. Tabernacle néoclassique.

18th century. Like Brunelleschi type florentine basilica. Neoclassical tabernacle.

XVIII. Jahrhundert. Folgt dem Typ der florentinischen Basilika von Brunelleschi Neuklassischer Tabernakel.

El Rosario

LUGAR DE «LAS RAICES» EN LA VILLA DE LA ESPERANZA.
LIEU-DIT «LAS RAICES» DANS LA VILLA DE LA ESPERANZA.
«LAS RAICES» IN LA ESPERANZA.
«LAS RAICES» GEGEND IN DER VILLA DE LA ESPERANZA.

Une a su valor natural de excelentes pinares el recuerdo histórico de una reunión militar en junio de 1936.

Unit à la qualité de ses excellentes pinèdes le souvenir historique d'une réunion militaire en juin 1936.

Consolidates its natural pine landscape values with the historic memory of a military meeting in June, 1936.

Vereint mit dem natürlichen Wert der hervorragenden Pinienwaelder, die historische Erinnerung an eine militaerische Zusammenkunft im Juni 1936.

1.2. MUSEOS
MUSEES
MUSEUMS
MUSEUM

Santa Cruz de Tenerife

MUSEO ARQUEOLOGICO.
MUSEE ARCHEOLOGIQUE.
ARCHEOLOGICAL MUSEUM.
ARCHAEOLOGISCHES MUSEUM.
Calle Bravo Murillo, s./n.

Contenido: Arqueología y Antropología canaria.

Contenu: Archéologie et Anthropologie des canaries.

Contents: Archeology and anthropology (Canary).

Inhalt: Archaeologie und janarische Anthropologie.

MUSEO MUNICIPAL «Antiguo Convento de San Francisco».
MUSEE MUNICIPAL. «Ancien Couvent de San Francisco».
MUNICIPAL MUSEUM. «Antiguo Convento de San Francisco».
STAEDTICHES MUSEUM. «Antiguo Convento de San Francisco».
Calle J. Murphy, s/n.

Contenido: Exclusivamente dedicado a pintura antigua, moderna y sobre todo local.

Contenu: Exclusivement dédié à la pinture, ancienne, moderne et surtout locale.

Contents: Dedicated exclusively to paintings; old, modern and above all local.

Inhalt: Ausschliesslich der alten, modernen und vor allem der lokalen Malerei gewidmet.

1.3. PARQUES Y JARDINES
PARCS ET JARDINS
PARKS AND GARDENS
PARK UND GARTENANLAGEN

La Orotava

PARQUE NACIONAL DEL TEIDE. A 53 km. de Santa Cruz de Tenerife.
PARC NATIONAL DU TEIDE. A 53 km. de Santa Cruz de Tenerife.
TEIDE NATIONAL PARK. 53 kilometers away from Santa Cruz de Tenerife.
NATIONAL PARK VON TEIDE 53 km von Santa Cruz de Tenerife entfernt.

Contenido: Taginaste, margarita y violeta del Teide, alelí y retama de Las Cañadas, cedro canario.

Contenu: «Taginaste», marguerite et violette du Teide, haleli et genêt de Las Cañadas, cèdre des canaries.

Contents: Taginaste, daisy and violet from Teide, winter gilliflower and broom from Las Cañadas, and Canary cedar.

Inhalt: Tagináste (leguminose Staude), Margeriten und Veilchen von Teide, Levkojen und Ginster von Las Cañadas, Kanarische Zeden.

El Paso

PARQUE NACIONAL DE LA CALDERA DE TABURIENTE.
PARC NATIONAL DE LA CALDERA DE TABURIENTE.
CALDERA DE TABURIENTE NATIONAL PARK.
NATIONALPARK DES KESSELS VON TABURIENTE.

Contenido: Barbuzano, codeso, faya, gacia, loro, tagasaste y taginaste. Cardones, chumberas y tebaibas. Acebos, adernos, brezos y marmolanes. Cabras cimarronas.

Contenu: «Barbuzano» (Apollonias Canariensis), «codeso» (espèce de trèfle), laurier de Portugal, «tagasaste» et «taginaste». Chardons, cactus et «tébaides». Houx, «adernos» bruyères et «marmolanes». Chèvres sauvages procédant des chèvres domestiques.

Contents: Barbuzano, hairy cytisus, Portuguese laurel, faya, gacia, tagasaste, taginaste. Canary spurge, Indian fig, tebaidas. Holly trees, heather, adernos, marmolanes. Wild goats.

Inhalt: Barbuzano (kanarischer Baum), Zytisus, Buchen, Gacia, Kirschlorbeerbaum, Tagasaste und Taginaste (leguminose Stauden): Disteln, Faigenkakteen und Tebaidas. Christdom, Aderno (kanarischer Baum) Heiderkraut und Marmoles. Wilde Ziegen.

Puerto de la Cruz

JARDIN DE ACLIMATACION DE LA OROTAVA.
JARDIN D'ACCLIMATATION DE LA OROTAVA.
ACLIMATIZED GARDEN OF LA OROTAVA.
AKKLIMATISIERUNGSGARTEN VON OROTAVA.
Pago del Durazno.

Contenido: Flora mundial, principalmente de zonas cálidas.

Contenu: Flore mondiale, principalement des pays chauds.

Contents: World flora, mainly from tropical zones.

Inhalt: Flora der ganzen Welt, hauptsaechlich der heissen Zonen.

1.4. BIBLIOTECAS
BIBLIOTHEQUES
LIBRAIRES
BIBLIOTHEKEN

En Santa Cruz de Tenerife

BIBLIOTECA MUNICIPAL. Plaza del Príncipe.

En La Laguna

BIBLIOTECA UNIVERSITARIA. Universidad de La Laguna.
BIBLIOTECA DE LA REAL SOCIEDAD DE AMIGOS DEL PAIS. Calle San Agustín.

En el Puerto de la Cruz

BIBLIOTECA DEL INSTITUTO DE ESTUDIOS HISPANICOS.

BIBLIOTECA INGLESA, en los Jardines del Hotel Taoro.

1.5. ARTESANIA
ARTISANAT
GRAFTWORK
KUNSTHANDWERK

Los objetos de artesanía pueden adquirirse en los principales comercios de las islas de esta especialidad.

Les objets d'artisanat peuvent être acquis dans les principaux commerces de cette spécialité.

Articles of this nature can be acquired in shops which specialize in these goods.

Kunstegewerbliche Gegenstände kann man in den Hauptgeschäften dieses Zweiges auf allen Insel erstehen.

Calados. Ajoures.
Lace. Durchbrochene Arbeiten.

En toda la isla de Tenerife, especialmente en la Villa de la Orotava, Puerto de la Cruz y los Realejos.

Dans toute l'île de Ténérife spécialement à la Villa de La Orotava, Puerto de la Cruz et los Realejos.

This can be obtained in all parts of the islandé but it is a speciality of La Orotava, Puerto de la Cruz and Los Realejos.

Auf der ganzen Insel Teneriffa, hauptsächlich in Villa de La Orotava, Puerto de la Cruz und Los Realejos, zu haben.

Bordados.
Broderies.
Embroidery.
Stickereien.

En la isla de La Palma.

Dans l'île de La Palma.

This is a speciality of La Palma Island.

Auf der Insel La Palma.

Hilanderas.
Filanderies.
Spun Yarn.
Spinnerei-Arbeiten.

En Tegueste y Taganana.

A Tegueste et Taganana.

In Tegueste and Taganana.

In Tegueste und Taganana.

Alfarería.
Poterie.
Pottery.
Töpferarbeiten.

En la Victoria de Acentejo, La Laguna y Santa Cruz de Tenerife.

A la Victoria de Acentejo, La Laguna et Santa Cruz de Tenerife.

It comee principally from Victoria de Acentejo, La Laguna and Santa Cruz de Tenerife.

In la Victoria de Acentejo, La Laguna und Santa Cruz de Tenerife.

Cestería. Panieries.
Basketwork. Flechtarbeiten.

En Bajamar, Los Realejos y otros lugares.

A Bajamar, Los Realejos et autres endroits.

A speciality of Bajamar, Los Realejos and some other places.

In Bajamar, Los Realejos und anderen Orten.

2. ALOJAMIENTOS
LOGEMENTS
ACCOMODATION
UNTERKUNFTE

2.1. HOTELES
HOTELS
HOTELS
HOTELS

Santa Cruz de Tenerife

MENCEY. José Naveira, 38. H*****.
BRUJA. Avda. de Bélgica, s/n. H****.
PARQUE. Méndez Núñez, 38. H****.
DIPLOMATICO. Antonio Nebrija, 6. H***.
ANAGA. Imeldo Seris, 7. H**.
PELINOR. Bethencourt Alfonso, 8. HR**.
TABURIENTE. Doctor Guigou, 19. HR**.
TAMAIDE. General Franco, 108. HR**
SAN JOSE. Santa Rosa de Lima, 7. H*
COLON RAMBLA. Viera y Clavijo, 4. RA***
PLAZA. Plaza de la Candelaria, 9. RA***
MIMOSAS. Enrique Wolfson, 36. RA**
CAPITOL. San Sebastián, 62. HR***
PECEÑO. Pilar, 5. HR***
TANAUSU. Padre Anchieta, 6. HR***
UCANCA. Cruz Verde, 24, HR***
MIRAMAR. Avda. de Anaga, 5. HR**
PADRON. General Mola, 112. HR**
RAMOS. Rambla de Pulido, 93. H**

Adeje

GRAN TINERFE. Playa de las Américas. H****
JARDIN TROPICAL. Urbanización San Eugenio. HA***
PARK HOTEL TROYA. Playa de las Américas. H***
PONDEROSA. Playa de las Américas. HA***
BORINQUEN. Playa de las Américas. RA**

Arona

BELROY. Los Cristianos, s/n. H***
TEN-BELL. Las Galletas. HA**
EUROPA. Playa de las Américas. H****
ORO NEGRO. C-G, 2. HA***

Bajamar

NAUTILUS La Comisa. H****
DELFIN-LAGUNA. La Comisa, s/n. H***
NEPTUNO. Ctra. Punta Hidalgo, km. 14. H***
TINGUARO. Urbanización Montemar. H***

Candelaria

TENERIFE TOUR. Las Caletillas, km. 17. H***
PUNTA DEL REY. Avda. Costera de Candelaria. H****
LOS GERANIOS. Los Geranios, 1. HA***

Las Cañadas del Teide

PARADOR NACIONAL CAÑADAS DEL TEIDE. Apartado 15 de la Orotava. H***

Cristianos (Los) (Arona)

REVERON. General Franco, 9. H**
PRINCESA DACIL. Avda. Principal de Penetración. HA***

El Medano

LOS VALOS. Playa del Medano. H**
CAREL. H**
EL MEDANO. Playa del Medano. H***

Puerto de la Cruz

BOTANICO. Avda. Richard J. Yeoward. H*****
LORO PARQUE. La Hacienda. H*****
SAN FELIPE. Avda. de Colón, 13. H*****
YBARRA SEMIRAMIS. Leopoldo Cologan, 12. H*****
ATALAYA GRAN HOTEL. Parque Taoro. H****
BONANZA CANARIFE. Urbanización La Paz. H****
ATLANTIS. Playa Martiánez, s/n. H****
CONCORDIA PLAYA. Avda. del Generalísimo, s/n. H****
DANIA PARK. Cupido, 17. H****
GRAN HOTEL LOS DOGOS. Urbanización Durazno. H*****
EDEN ESPLANADE. Urbanización S. Fernando. RA****
EUROTEL INTERPALACE. La Paz, 13. H****
FLORIDA TENERIFE. Avda. Blas Pérez González. H****
MAGEC. Cupido, 11. H****
MARTIANEZ. Generalísimo, 19. H****
MELIA PUERTO DE LA CRUZ. Avda. Marqués de Villanueva. H*****
OROTAVA GARDEN. Avda. Aguilar y Quesada, s/n. H****
PARQUE SAN ANTONIO. Ctra. Las Arenas, s/n. H****
LA PAZ. Urbanización La Paz. H****
QUEBEY. Agustín de Bethencourt, 18 HR****
TENERIFE PLAYA. Avda. Colón, 12. H****
TIGAICA. Parque del Taoro, 16 H****
EL TOPE. Calzada de Martiánez, s/n. H****
LAS VEGAS. Avda. de Colón, 2. H****
YBARRA VALLE MAR. Avda. de Colón, 2. H****
LAS AGUILAS. Las Arenas. H***
EL BAJIO. Paseo Luis Lavaggi, s/n. HR***
BELAIR. Valois, 18. HA***
CASA DEL SOL. Urbanización San Fernando. H***
COLON. Urbanización La Paz. HR***
CONDESA. Quintana, 13. HR***
CHIMISAY. Bethencourt, 14. HR***
LA CHIRIPA. Urbanización San Fernando. HA***
DON JUAN. Puerto Viejo, 56. H***
DON MANOLITO. Lomo de los Guirres. H***
GUAJARA. Generalísimo, s/n. HA***
HARAL. José Antonio, 3. HR***
IKARUS. Urbanización La Paz. H***
INTERNACIONAL. Ctra. Las Arenas, 91. H***
LAVAGGI. Generalísimo, s/n. RA***
MARQUESOL. Esquivel, 3. HR***
MARTE. Dr. Ingram, 22. H***
MARTINA. Generalísimo, 1. HA***
MIRAMAR. Parque de Taoro. H***
MONNALISA. Pérez Zamora, 2. H***
MONOPOL. Quintana, 15. H***
NOPAL. José Antonio, 17. H***
ONUBA. Blanco, 15. HR***
LOS PRINCIPES. Dr. Víctor Pérez, s/n. H***
SAN BORONDON. Puerto Viejo, 4. H***
SAN TELMO. San Telmo, 18. H***
TAGOR. Virtud, 3. HR***
TEIDEMAR. Urbanización La Paz. RA***
TROPICAL. Pl. Gral. Franco, 9. HR***
TROVADOR. Puerto Viejo, 40. H***
VICTORIA. Prolongación Puerto Viejo. HR***
XIBANA PARK. Valois, 25. H***
BELGICA. Avda. Colón, 11. HR**
CAPRICHO. Dinamarca, 8. HR**
ESQUILON. San Antonio, 13. HR**
FLORALVA. Calvo Sotelo, 17. RA**
FRAMPEREZ. José Arroyo, 4. HR**
GUACIMARA. Bethencourt, 9. HR**
MARQUESA. Quintana, 11. H**
ORO NEGRO. Avda. Colón, 14. H**
PICAFLOR. Ctra. del Botánico, 6. RA**
PINOCHO. Esquilón, s/n. HR**
PUERTO AZUL. Lomo, 28. HR**

SAN AMARO. Urbanización La Paz, 41. HR**
TEJEUMA. Pérez Zamora, 51. HR**
AREA. Dr. Ingram, 15. HR**
AROSA. Esquivel, 10. HR**
BUNGE. Avda. Venezuela, 1. HR**
EDUA. Mazaroco, 16. HR**
LOS GERANIOS. Lomo, 21. HR**
LOLY. Sala, 2. HR**
MARBELLA. Lomo, 30. HR**
LAS MERCEDES. Iriarte, 31. HR**
PLATANERA. Blanco, 31. HR**
PLAZA Pl. Gral. Franco, 11. HR**
TAMARA. Bethencourt, 35. HR**
TARAJAL. José Antonio, 20. HR**
VIMA. Santo Domingo, 4. HR**

Puerto Santiago (Santiago del Teide)

LOS GIGANTES. Gigantes. H****

Los Realejos

LA ROMANTICA. Urbanización La Romántica. RA**
REFORMA. Urbanización Tierra de Oro. H***

Tacoronte

LOGIS CHAMPAGNE. Mesa del Mar. RA**
MAR Y SOL. Mesa del Mar. HA***

San Sebastián de la Gomera

PARADOR NACIONAL DE LA GOMERA. H***
GARAJONAY. Ruiz de Padrón, 17. HR**

Santa Cruz de la Palma

PARADOR NACIONAL DE SANTA CRUZ. Avda. Blas Pérez González, 8. H***
MAYANTIGO. Alvarez Abréu, 8. H***
CANARIAS. A. Cabrera Pinto, 27. HR**

2.2. APARTAMENTOS TURISTICOS
APPARTEMENTS TOURISTIQUES
TOURIST APARTMENTS
APARTEMENTHAUSER

BAHIA CLUB. Avda. de Anaga, s/n. Lujo.
PARQUE. Gral. Franco, 106. 2.ª C.
VISTA MAR. Playa San Marcos. Sindicatos (Icod). 2.ª C.
MENENDEZ. Bethencourt Alfonso, 18-20.

Adeje

BUNGAMERICA. Playa de América. 1.ª C.
VERACRUZ. Playa de las Américas. 1.ª C.

Arona

CRISTIANMAR. Del Coronel o Avda. de Suecia-Los Cristianos. 2.ª C.
ROSAMAR. Los Cristianos. 3.ª C.

Bajamar (La Laguna)

BELLAMAR. Ctra. General. 1.ª C.
MARYFLOR. Ctra. General. 1.ª C.
PIEDRA, LA. Ctra. General. 1.ª C.
SEA SIDE. El Alto-Urb. González Vernetta. 2.ª C.

3. GASTRONOMIA
GASTRONOMIE
GASTRONOMY
GASTRONOMIE

3.1. RESTAURANTES
RESTAURANTS
RESTAURANTS
RESTAURANTS

Santa Cruz de Tenerife

LA POSADA. Veinticinco de Julio, 6 y 8. 1.ª C.
BAVIERA. General Franco, 42. 2.ª C.
CASA RAMOS. Rambla de Pulido, 95. 2.ª C.
LA ESTANCIA. Méndez Núñez, 110. 2.ª C.
GAMBRINUS. Adelantado, 1. 2.ª C.
HONG KONG CHINA. General Franco, 141. 2.ª C.
MANROVI. Bethencourt Alfonso, 6 y 8. 2.ª C.
EL SOTOMAYOR. José Murphy, 4. 2.ª C.
TABURIENTE. Dr. Guigou, 19. 2.ª C.
ATLANTICO. Marina, 1. 3.ª C.
AVENIDA. Avda. José Antonio, 10. 3.ª C.
BAILEN. Imeldo Seris, 108. 3.ª C.
CUATRO NACIONES. José Murphy, 1. 3.ª C.
CHINA. Avda. de Anaga, s/n. 3.ª C.
GALLO ROJO. General Franco, 27. 3.ª C.
MERINO. Doctor Allart, 23. 3.ª C.
MIMOSAS. Enrique Wolfson, 16. 3.ª C.
PORTON DE ORO. General Franco, 30. 3.ª C.
EL PORVENIR. Castillo, 62. 3.ª C.
STOP. Avda. La Salle, 18. 3.ª C.
TIERRA MIA. María Jiménez. 3.ª C.
VALENCIA. Avda. Anaga, s/n. 3.ª C.

Adeje

EL CORRAL DEL GUANCHE. Carretera general Tijoco. 2.ª C.

Arona

LA BALLENA. Costa del Silencio. 2.ª C.
BAHIA. Explanada del Muelle. 3.ª C.
SANTA ANARA. Urb. Santa Ana. 3.ª C.
JARDIN CANARIO. Las Galletas. 4.ª C.
NAPOLEON. Las Galletas. 4.ª C.

Bajamar

LA CAMPANA. Urb. Vernetta. 2.ª C.
ATLANTICO. El Barranco, s/n. 3.ª C.

EL GALLEGO. Ctra. General, s/n. 3.ª C.
MARGARITA. La Rambla, s/n. 3.ª C.
EL YATE. Avda. del Sol, s/n. 3.ª C.
SHERIFF. La Fonda, s/n. 4.ª C.

Candelaria

CASA SINDO. Obispo Pérez Cáceres, 12. 3.ª C.
PLAYAMAR. Obispo Pérez Cáceres, s/n. 3.ª C.
SOL Y PLAYA. Las Caletillas. 3.ª C.
CAN CATALA. Obispo Pérez Cáceres, 2. 4.ª C.
PEDRO REVISOR. Obispo Pérez Cáceres, 5. 4.ª C.
PISCINA MUNICIPAL. Candelaria. 4.ª C.

Cristianos (Los)

GUAYERO. Playa de Los Cristianos. 1.ª C.
CRISTIANMAR. Los Cristianos. 2.ª C.
LINARES. General Franco, 19. 2.ª C.
DON CARLOS. Juan XXIII, s/n. 3.ª C.
CRISTINA. 1.ª transv. Avda. General Franco. 3.ª C.
MALAGA. La Playa. 3.ª C.
PIZZERIA MARIA DEL MAR. Edificio Guayeró. 3.ª C.
FORTUNA. Juan, 23. 4.ª C.
PARRILLA. Avda. General Franco, s/n. 4.ª C.

Cuesta (La)

BOMBA H. Ctra. de La Cuesta, s/n. 4.ª C.
EL REY DE LOS PINCHOS. Villa Concepción, 11. 4.ª C.

Esperanza (La)

CAÑADAS. Carretera general, km. 7,5. 3.ª C.
RAICES. Ctra. La Cañada, km. 10. 3.ª C.

Garachico

SIOUX. Rep. Venezuela, 1. 3.ª C.

Granadilla

DOS HERMANOS. Calvario, 21. 3.ª C.
GARIGONZA. Carretera general, s/n. 3.ª C.
MAGALLANES. Médano, s/n. 3.ª C.
AVENCIO. El Médano. 4.ª C.
SANTIAGO. Carretera general, s/n. 4.ª C.

Guancha (La)

TRES MUÑECAS. Santo Domingo, s/n. 4.ª C.

Güimar

CASA ELOY. Puertito de Güimar. 3.ª C.
MOBY DICK. El Puertito. 3.ª C.
NEPTUNO. El Puertito. 4.ª C.

Icod

BALNEARIO. Playa de San Marcos. 3.ª C.
GLORIA. Rambla Pérez del Cristo. 3.ª C.
BODEGON PLAYA. Playa de San Marcos. 4.ª C.
BODEGON CIRA. Playa San Marcos. 4.ª C.
PUERTO DE SAN MARCOS. Playa de San Marcos. 4.ª C.

Laguna (La)

AEROPUERTO. Los Rodeos, s/n. 1.ª C.
COUNTRY CLUB DE PARIS. Camino de San Bartolomé, s/n. 1.ª C.
ALEGRANZA. La Somada Tejina, s/n. 3.ª C.
EL QUE FALTABA. Castillo, s/n. 3.ª C.
ETZE-ANDIA. Ctra. general Norte-Guamasa, s/n. 3.ª C.
PADRON. Núñez de la Peña, 19. 3.ª C.
RANCHO GRANDE. Camino del Medio, 15. 3.ª C.
ROMANTICO. Primera, 19. 3.ª C.
LA TABERNA. Fdez. de la Cruz, s/n. 3.ª C.
CASA ANTONIO. Plaza San Francisco, 7. 4.ª C.

Matanza

LOS AMIGOS. Ctra. general, km. 105. 4.ª C.
BODEGON MOCAN. Ctra. general, km. 25. 4.ª C.
CASA PADILLA. Ctra. general, km. 26,5. 4.ª C.
EL NEGUS. Ctra. general, km. 25,7. 4.ª C.

Médano (El)

FAMILIAR. El Médano, s/n. 3.ª C.
PATIO MEDANO. Ctra. El Médano, s/n. 3.ª C.

Orotava (La)

MESON DEL TEIDE. Portillo de las Cañadas del Teide. 2.ª C.
OROTAVA. Tomás Calamita, s/n. 3.ª C.
EL PORTILLO. Ctra. Dorsal, km. 32, 3.ª C.
TEIDE. El Portillo. 3.ª C.
CASA JUANITO. El Ramal. 4.ª C.
ONELLA. Dr. Domingo González, 42. 4.ª C.

Puerto de la Cruz

BELLAVISTA. Urbanización La Paz. 1.ª C.
CASA CHOP SUEY. Calvo Sotelo, 51. 1.ª C.
HOSTERIA CASTILLO DE SAN FELIPE. Castillo de San Felipe. 1.ª C.
PLAYA. Avda. de Colón, s/n. 1.ª C.
BAMBI. Lomito, s/n. 2.ª C.
BUFFET TOSCA. José Antonio, 1. 2.ª C.
GRANADA. San Felipe, 41. 2.ª C.
LA HERRERIA. Cologón, 7. 2.ª C.
LA ISLA. Valois, 49. 2.ª C.
OASIS. Avda. Venezuela, 3. A. 2.ª C.
PAVILLON. Explanada Martínez. 2.ª C.
PEÑON. Puerto Viejo, s/n. 2.ª C.
SAN BORONDON. Urbanización San Borondón. 2.ª C.
SAN MIGUEL. Del Pozo, s/n. 2.ª C.
SANCHO PANZA. Iriarte, 36. 2.ª C.
TIROL. Avda. Gral. Franco, s/n. 2.ª C.
VICTORIA. San Borondón, s/n. 2.ª C.

Punta del Hidalgo

LA PERLA. Urbanización Tessessinte. 2.ª C.
ALTAGAY CLUB. Urbanización Tessessinte. 3.ª C.
CASA TITA. Ctra. general Punta del Hidalgo, s/n. 4.ª C.

Realejos

CUEVA GRILL. La Romántica, 2. A. 2.ª C.
TIERRA DE ORO. Urbanización Montañeta. 2.ª C.
CLUB ROMANTICA. La Romántica. 3.ª C.
LA RANA. Avda. Santiago Apóstol, 30. 3.ª C.
LA ROMANTICA. Urbanización La Romántica. 3.ª C.
LOS FAROLES. La Longuera. 4.ª C.
LA FINCA. Ctra. general La Longuera, s/n. 4.ª C.
LOS HERMANOS. El Tosal, s/n. 4.ª C.
EL TOSCAL. El Toscal, s/n. 4.ª C.

Rodeos (Los)

CASA RAMALLO. Ctra. general, km. 13. 4.ª C.

Rosario (El)

CASA BELISARIO. Ctra. La Esperanza, km. 6. 3.ª C.
SUMIVA. Parque Residencial Tabaiba. 3.ª C.
CONSUELO. Ctra. general Sur, km. 10. 4.ª C.
MERENDERO LEON. Ctra. Las Cañadas, km. 8. 4.ª C.

Santa Ursula

LAGAR TAMAIDE. Ctra. general, s/n. 2.ª C.
LOS CORALES. Cuesta de la Villa. 3.ª C.
MESON SAN ANTONIO. Carretera del Pinito, s/n. 3.ª C.
OSCAR. Ctra. Norte, km. 32,300. 3.ª C.
EL PAJAR. Cuesta de la Villa. 3.ª C.
CASA ESPERANZA. Cuesta de la Villa. 4.ª C.

Santiago del Teide

BAMBOO BAR. Urb. Acantilado Los Gigantes. 3.ª C.
SOL Y ARENA. Playa de la Arena. 3.ª C.
PANCHO. Playa de la Arena-Puerto de Santiago. 4.ª C.

Sauzal

MESON LA CABAÑA. Ctra. general Norte, km. 21. 3.ª C.
CASA VALENCIA. Ctra. general, km. 20. 4.ª C.

Tacoronte

FIESTA CANARIA. Barrio Santa Catalina. 1.ª C.
LA GAVIOTA. Mesa del Mar. 2.ª C.
LOS LIMONEROS. Ctra. general, s/n. 3.ª C.
LA TAURINA. Ctra. del Norte, km. 18. 3.ª C.
AQUI ESTA EL DETALLE. Ctra. del Norte. 4.ª C.
BODEGON GARAJONAY. Ctra. general, 188. 4.ª C.
LAS CUEVAS. El Cantillo. 4.ª C.

Tegueste

CASA HORTENSIA. Ctra. general a Tejina, km. 7. 4.ª C.
JUAN CRUZ. Ctra. general, km. 7. 4.ª C.

3.2. ESPECIALIDADES GASTRONOMICAS
   SPECIALITE GASTRONOMIQUES
   GASTRONOMIC SPECIALITIES
   SPEZIALITATEN

Caldo de pescado. Cazuela tinerfeña.
Papas arrugadas con varias clases de «mojo» (salsa).
Viejas cocidas, «mojo» picón.
Cabrillas fritas a la portuense.
Chicharros rellenos.
Cabrito asado.
Cerdo salvaje asado (Isla de La Gomera).
Chicharros.
Morcillas dulces.

Bouillon de poisson. Casserole ténérifienne.
Pommes de terre «ridées» avec diverses sortes de sauces.
Viejas cocidas, «mojo» picon.
Poissons frits.
«Chicharros» farcis.
Chevreau rôti.
Cochon sauvage rôti.
Chicharros.
Boudins doux.

TYPICAL DISHES. Caldo de pescado (Fish Soup). Cazuela Tinerfeña.
«Mojo» Picón.
Cabrillas fritas a la portuense.
Chicharros.
Cabrito asado (Roast Goat).
Cerdo salvaje asado (Roast Wild boar - a speciality of La Gomera Island), and morcillas dulces.

Caldo de pescado (Fischsuppe). Cazuela tinerfeña.
Papas arrugadas («runzelige» Kartoffeln) mit mehreren Arten von Sossen (mojo).
Viejas cocidas, «mojo» picón (Spezialsosse).
Cabrillas fritas a la portuense.
Chicharros rellenos (gefüllte Fische).
Cabrito asado (gebratenes Zicklein).
Cerdo salvaje asado (Wildschweinbraten), auf der Insel Gomera.
Chicharros (Fische).
Morcillas dulces (süsse Blutwurst).

Postres
Desserts
Desserts
Süsstspeisen

Turrón de «gofio» (harina de maíz o trigo tostado).
Higos chumbos «Bienmesabe».
Cuellos de almendras.
Quesadilla de El Hierro.
Rapaduras de la Palma (hechas de gofio y miel de caña).
Pasteles navideños de La Laguna y del Puerto de la Cruz.
Queso blanco de fabricación casera de El Hierro, La Palma y Sur de Tenerife.

Turrón de «gofio» (farine de maïs ou blé grillé).
Figues «Bienmesabe».
Cous d'amandes.
Quesadilla de El Hierro.
Rapaduras de la Palma (faites de gofio et miel de canne).
Gâteaux de Noël de La Laguna et Puerto de la Cruz.
Fromage blanc de fabrication artisanale d'El Hierro, La Palma et Sud de Ténérife.

Typical sweets are Turrón de Gofio.
Higos Chumbos (Prickly Pears).
Cuellos de Almendras (Almonds).
Quesadilla de El Hierro (Chesecake).
Rapaduras de la Palma.
Christmas Cakes of La Laguna and Puerto de la Cruz, and homemade cheese from La Palma, El Hierro and the south of Tenerife Island.

Turrón de gofio (Kuchen aus Maismehl oder geröstetem Weizen).
Higos chumbos «Bienmesabe» (Kaktusfeigen).
Cuellos de almendras (Mandelkragen).
Quesadilla von der Insel Hierro.
Rapaduras von der Insel La Palma, hergestellt aus geröstetem Weizen mehl und Zuckerrohr-Honing.
Pasteles navideños (Weihnachtskuchen) aus La Laguna und Puerto de la Cruz. Weisser Hausmacher-Käse von der Insel Hierro, La Palma und aus dem Süden.

Vinos del país
Vin du pays
Local wines
Weine des Landes

Tenerife y las demás islas producen excelentes vinos de mesa, blanco y tinto, y tienen fama universal su malvasía y moscatel.

Ténérife et les autres îles produisent d'excellents vins de table blancs et rouges; la malvoisie et le muscat ont une réputation mondiale.

Tenerife and the islands produce excellent red and white wines, Muscatel and Malvasía being the most wellknown.

Sowohl Teneriffa als auch die-Übrigen Inseln bringen vortreffliche Tischweine (Rot- und Weissweine) hervor. Weltberühmt sind der Malvasier und Muskateller-Wein.

4. AGENDA PRACTICA
AGENDA PRATIQUE
PRATICAL AGENDA
PRAKTISCHES NACHSCHLAGEWERK

4.1. CONSULADOS
   CONSULATS
   CONSULATES
   KONSULATE

AUSTRIA. San Francisco, 17.
BELGICA. San Pedro de Alcántara, 11.
BOLIVIA. L. Vega, 6.
CHILE. Juan A. Delgado, 7.
DINAMARCA. Avda. Anaga, 43.
FINLANDIA. Avda. Anaga, 43.
FRANCIA. Méndez Núñez, 22.
GRAN BRETAÑA. S. Guerra, 40.
ITALIA. B. Alfonso, 19.
LIBERIA. B. Alfonso, 25.
MONACO. Pilar, 14.
NORUEGA. Doctor Zerolo, 14.
PAISES BAJOS. Marina, 9.
PANAMA. Puerta Canseco, 47.
PORTUGAL. Velázquez, 11.
PARAGUAY. Rambla Gral. Franco, 55.
URUGUAY. 25 de Julio, 15.
VENEZUELA. Pilar, 25.

4.2. DIRECCIONES Y SERVICIOS UTILES
   ADRESSES ET SERVICES UTILES
   USEFUL ADDRESSES AND SERVICES
   NOTZLICHE ADRESSEN UND DIENSTE

Correos, telégrafos y teléfonos.
Telegraphes et telephones
Post and telegraph office and telephone exchange
Post-und Telegraphenamt

Santa Cruz de Tenerife

Plaza de España.

La Laguna

Plaza de España.

Puerto de la Cruz
Agustín Bethencourt, 15.

Santa Cruz de la Palma
Plaza del Muelle, 2.

Comunicaciones
Communications
Communications
Verkehrsverbindungen

Líneas aéreas
Lignes aériennes
Air routes
Fluglinien

Información: Avda. Anaga, 23.
Servicios directos o combinados con los principales aeropuertos nacionales y extranjeros.

Information: Avda. Anaga, 23.
Services directs ou en correspondance avec les principaux aéroports nationaux et internationaux.

Information: Avda. Anaga, 23.
Direct or combined to the main domestic and foreign airports.

Information: Avda. Anaga, 23.
Direktverbindungen oder Anschlüsse zu den wichtigsten in- und ausländischen Flughäfen.

Líneas marítimas
Lignes maritimes
Sea routes
Schiffslinien

Información: Marina, 59.
Servicios directos o combinados con el resto de las islas del Archipiélago, así como con la península, Baleares y Africa.

Information: Marina, 59.
Services directs ou en correspondance avec les autres îles de l'archipel, avec la péninsule, les Baléares et l'Afrique.

Information: Marina, 59.
Direct or combined to the other islands in the Archipelago as well as to Mainland Spain, the Balearic Islands and Africa.

Information: Marina, 59.
Direktverbindungen oder Anschlüsse zu den anderen Inseln des Archipels, sowie zur Halbinsel, den Balearen und Afrika.

4.3. CLIMA-CLIMAT
CLIMATE-KLIMAT

Por las tablas meteorológicas puede observarse que sólo hay una pequeña variación de temperatura durante el año debido a que en el invierno la corriente del Golfo calienta la atmósfera, y en el verano los vientos alisios la refrescan. Según datos tomados en Santa Cruz, la presión media al nivel del mar es, todos los meses, superior al normal de 1.013 milibares, (ó 760 mm.), lo cual es consecuencia del predominio de las condiciones anticiclónicas. Que el máximo de presión se presente (al nivel del mar) en enero, concuerda con el hecho de ser precisamente en este mes cuando el centro del anticiclón atlántico ocupa su posición más meridional. En general, son de hasta 1.030 milibares, y los mínimos, de 990, lo que supone una variación total de 40 milibares, muy pequeña si se compara con las variaciones absolutas de la zona templada, de hasta 125 milibares.

El régimen de lluvias muestra un gran contraste en su distribución, pues la cantidad anual de lluvias varía desde menos de 100 mm., en las zonas secas, hasta más de 750 mm., en las más lluviosas. Esto es consecuencia del gran papel que juega la configuración orográfica. La nieve sólo se manifiesta en las cumbres, muy raramente a niveles inferiores a 1.700 metros, y prácticamente nunca por debajo de los 1.200. En Izaña, el número medio de días de nieve al año es de 11, que pueden ser desde el 15 de octubre al 15 de mayo. Algunas nevadas son importantes, llegando a alcanzar la nieve más de un metro de espesor y manteniéndose varios días. Por término medio, en Las Cañadas, el suelo está cubierto de nieve 15 días al año. Nieves perpetuas no existen a ninguna altura, pues incluso en el Teide hay muchos inviernos en que durante períodos de varias semanas la nieve sólo se mantiene en cavidades y lugares muy resguardados.

On peut observer sur les tables météorologiques qu'il y a seulement une petite variation de température pendant l'année à cause du fait que, en hiver, le courant du Golf réchauffe l'atmosphère et qu'en été, les vents alizés la rafraîchissent. D'après les données prises à Santa Cruz, la pression moyenne au niveau de la mer est, tous les mois, supérieure à la normale de 1013 mb (ou 760 mm) ce qui est une conséquence de la prédominance des conditions anticycloniques.
Que le maximum de pression (au niveau de la mer) se présente en janvier, ce qui concorde avec le fait que c'est précisément pendant ce mois que le centre de l'anticyclone atlantique occupe sa position la plus méridionale; en général, les maxima sont de 1030 mb et les minima de 990 mb ce qui suppose une variation totale de 40 millibares très petite si on la compare avec les variations absolues de la zone tempérée, qui vont jusqu'à 125 mb.
Le régime de pluies montre un grand contraste dans sa distribution, car la quantité annuelle

de pluies varie de moins de 100 mm dans les zones sèches jusqu'à plus de 750 mm dans les pluvieuses. C'est la conséquence du grand rôle que joue la configuration orographique. La neige ne se manifeste que sur les sommets, très rarement à des niveaux inférieurs à 1700 mètres et pratiquement jamais au-dessous 1200 mètres. A Izaña, le nombre moyen de jours de neige par an est de 11 qui peuvent aller du 15 octobre au 15 mai. Quelques chutes de neige sont importantes, la neige arrivant à atteindre un mètre d'épaisseur et durer plusieurs jours. En moyenne, à Las Cañadas, le sol est couvert de neige 15 jours par an. Les neiges éternelles n'existent à aucune altitude car même sur le Teide il y a beaucoup d'hivers où, pendant des périodes de plusieurs semaines, la neige ne demeure que dans les cavités et lieux très abrités.

Meteorological tables tell us that throughout the whole year there are only small differences of temperature; this is due to the fact that during the winter the Gulf Stream warms the atmosphere, whilst in summer there are the cooling effects of the east winds.

According to records of atmospheric conditions kept for Santa Cruz, the average pressure at sea level is, for all months, higher than the normal of 1,013 mb. (or 760 mm.) owing to the predominance of anticyclonic conditions. The highest pressure at sea level is recorded in January, which coincides with the fact that it is precisely in this month that the Atlantic anticyclone occupies its most southerly position. In general, there is a maximum of 1,030 mb. and a minimum of 990 mb; this varistion of 40 millibars is very small when compared with the absolute variations of up to 125 millibars in the temperate zone. The annual reinfall varies greatly from one region to another; in the driest areas it is less than 100 mm., whilst in the wettest it can be up to 750 mm., differences which are largely caused by their positions relative to the mountains. Snow only falls on the peaks, very seldon at levels below 1,700 metres, and almost never below 1,200 metres. In Izaña there are an average of 11 days of snow a year; some falls can be heavy, the depth sometimes being more than a metre and the snow lastigg for several days; they may take place between October 15th and May 15th. On average Las Cañadas is covered with snow for 15 days a year. There are no peaks which are covered with snow throughout the year, and in many, winters even Teide has only patches of snow in secluded spots for many weeks.

An Had der Klimatabellen kann man feststellen, dass die Temperaturen zwischen den einzelnen Jahreszeiten nur sehr wenig schwanken, was im Winter dem Golfstrom zuzuschreilben ist, der die Atmosphäre erwärmt und im Som-

mer den Passatwinden, die frische und kühle Luft heranbringen. Nach den in Santa Cruz aufgeommenen Daten ist der durchschnittliche Luftdruck in allen Monaten höher als 1.013 mb. (oder 760 mm.), da hier ein Hochdruckgebiet vorherrscht. Der höchste Luftdruck besteht im Januar, wenn das Zentrum des atlantischen Hochdruckgebietes sich weiter südlich verlagert. Im allgemeinen varriiert der Luftdruck zwischen 990 bis 1.030 mb., was eine Schwankung von 40 mb. bedeutet. Diese ist geringfügig, wenn man sie se ist geringfügig, wenn man sie mit den in der gemässigten Zone auftretenden Luftdruckschwankungen vergleicht, die bis zu 125 mb. ausmachen.
Die Menge der jährlichen Niederschläge in den einzelnen Zonen variiert zwischen 100 mm. in den trokkenen und über 750 mm. in den regenreichen Gebieten. Diese grosse Differenz hat ihre Ursache in den Höhenunterschieden auf der Insel. Schnee kommt nur auf den Berggipfeln vor, sehr selten in Höhen unter 1.700 m. und nie unter 1.200 m. In Izaña fällt im Durchschnitt an 11 Tagen im Jahr Schnee, die immer zwischen dem 15. Oktober und 15. Mai liegen. Einige Schneefälle sind von Bedeutung; hierbei erreicht der Schnee eine Dicke von über 1 m. und bleibt mehrere Tage liegen. Durchschnittlich ist der Boden an 15 Tagen im Jahr mit Schnee bedeckt. Fortdauernde Schneemassen gibt es in keinem Teil der Insel, denn sogar auf dem Teide gibt es Winter, in denen sich der Schnee nur in den Höhlungen und sehr geschützten Plätzen wochenlang hält.

Finalmente, cabe señalar los siguientes datos: ESTACION DE IZAÑA (2.367 m/a). Enero: Temperatura media, 3,8°, media de las máximas, 7,3°; media de las mínimas, 0,9°; oscilación media, 17°; media de las máximas, 21,8°; media de las mínimas, 13°; oscilación media, 8,8°.

Finalement, il faut signaler les données suivantes: STATION DE IZAÑA (2367 m/a). Janvier: Température moyenne, 3,8°; thermique maxima: 7,3°; thermique minima: 0,9°; oscillation thermique: 6,4°; Mois d'août: température moyenne 17°; thermique maxima: 21,8°; thermique minima: 13°; oscilation thermique, 8,8°.

IZAÑA METEOROLOGICAL STATION (2,367 m/a). January: Average temp. 3.8° C.; average max. temp. 7.3° C.; average min. temp. 0.9° C. August: Average temp. 17° C; average max. temp. 21.8° C.; average min. temp. 13° C.); average swing 8.8° C.

Zum Schluss folgende Daten: WETTERWARTE VON IZAÑA (2.367 m. hoch). Januar: Durchschnittstemperatur 3,8°; mittlere Höchsttemperatur 7,3°; mitlere Tiefsttemperatur 0,9°; durchschnittliche Schwankung 17°. August: Mittlere Höchsttemperatur 21,8°; mittlere Tiefst-

temperatur 13°; durchschnittliche Schwankung 8,8°.

ESTACION DE LA LAGUNA (547 m/a). Mes de enero: Temperatura media, 12,3°, media de las máximas, 15,5°, media de las mínimas, 8,8°; oscilación media, 6,7°. Mes de agosto: Temperatura media 21,1°; media de las máximas, 25,8°; media de las mínimas, 16,2°; oscilación media, 9,6°.

STATION DE LA LAGUNA (546 m/a). Mois de janvier: température moyenne, 12,3°. Thermique maxima, 15,5°. Thermique minima, 8,8°. Oscillation thermique, 6,7°. Mois d'août: température moyenne: 21,1°. Thermique maxima, 25,8. Thermique minima, 16,2°; Oscillation thermique 9,6°.

LA LAGUNA METEOROLOGICAL STATION (547 m/a). January: Av. temp. 12.3° C.; av. max. temp. 15.5° C.; av. min. temp. 8.8° C.; av. swing 6.7° C. August: av. temp. 21.1° C.; av. max. temp. 25.8° C.; av. min. temp. 16.2° C.; average swing 9.6° C.

WETTERWARTE VON LA LAGUNA (547 m. hoch). Januar: Durchschnittstemperatur 12,3°; mittlere Höchsttemperatur 15,5°; mittlere Tiefsttemperatur 8,8°; durchschnittliche Schwankung 6,7°. August: Durchschnittstemperatur 21,1°; mittlere Höchsttemperatur 25,8°; mittlere Tiefsttemperatur 16,2°; durchschnittliche Schwankung 9,6°.

ESTACION DE SANTA CRUZ (37 m/a). Mes de enero: Temperatura media 17,5°; media de las máximas, 20,4°; media de las mínimas, 14,7°; oscilación media, 5,7°. Mes de agosto: Temperatura media 25,2°; media de las máximas, 29,3°; media de las mínimas, 21,1°; oscilación media, 8,2°.
El agua de Tenerife puede beberse en cualquier parte de la isla con toda seguridad. En la isla no hay reptiles, ni animales feroces.

*STATION DE SANTA CRUZ (37 m/a). Mois de janvier: température moyenne, 17,5°. Thermique maxima, 20,4°. Thermique minima, 14,7°. Oscillation moyenne, 5,7°. Mois d'août: température moyenne, 25,2°. Thermique maxima, 29,3°. Thermique minima, 21,1°. Oscillation, 8,2°.
L'eau de Ténérife peut se boire dans n'importe quelle partie de l'île en toute sécurité. Dans l'île il n'y a ni des reptiles ni d'animaux sauvages.*

SANTA CRUZ METEOROLOGICAL STATION (37 m/a). January: Av. temp. 17.5° C., av. max. temp. 20.4° C.; av. min. temp. 14.7° C.; average swing 6.7° C. August: av. temp. 25.2° C.; av. max. temp. 29.3° C.; av. min. temp. 21.1° C.; average swing 8.2° C.
The water of Tenerife can be drunk in any part of the island with complete safety. There are no reptiles of wild animals on the island.

*WETTERWARTE VON SANTA CRUZ (37 m. hoch). Januar: Durchschnittstemperatur 17,5°; mittlere Höchsttemperatur 20,4°; mittlere Tiefsttemperatur 14,7°; durchschnittliche Schwankung 5,7°. August: Durchschnittstemperatur 25,2°; mittlere Höchsttemperatur 29,3°; mittlere Tiefsttemperatur 21,1°; durchschnittliche Schwankung 8,2°.
Das Wasser kann auf Teneriffa an jedem. Ort ohne weiteres getrunken werden. Auf der Insel gibt es weder Reptile noch wilde Tiere.*

**Temperaturas medias en Tenerife
Temperatures moyennes à Tenerife
Average temperatures of Tenerife
Mittlere Temperaturen auf Teneriffa**

Meses	Grados C
Enero	17,4
Febrero	17,0
Marzo	19,1
Abril	18,7
Mayo	20,3
Junio	22,3
Julio	23,9
Agosto	24,8
Septiembre	23,8
Octubre	23,5
Noviembre	21,7
Diciembre	18,5

Horas de sol: 3.000 al año.

Mois	*Degrés C*
Janvier	*17,4*
Février	*17,0*
Mars	*19,1*
Avril	*18,7*
Mai	*20.3*
Juin	*22,3*
Juillet	*23,9*
Août	*24,8*
Septembre	*23,8*
Octobre	*23,5*
Novembre	*21,7*
Décembre	*18,5*

Heures de soleil: 3000 par an.

Months	Grades C
January	17.4
February	17.0
March	19.1
April	18.7
May	20.3
June	22.3
July	23.9
August	24.8
September	23.8
October	23.5
November	21.7
December	18.5

Hours of sun: 3.000 a year.

Monat	Grad C
Januar	17,4
Februar	17,0
März	19,1
April	18,7
Mai	20,3
Juni	22,3
Juli	23,9
August	24,8
September	23,8
Oktober	23,5
November	21,7
Dezember	18,5

Anzahl der Sonnenstunden im Jahr: 3.000.

Alturas de la isla de Tenerife
Altitudes de l'ile de Tenerife
Highest peaks on the island of Tenerife
Höhen auf der Insel Teneriffa

Pico del Teide: 3.716 metros.
Chahorra (Pico Viejo): 3.016 metros.
Guajara: 2.790 metros.
Montaña Blanca: 2.743 metros.
El Sombrerito: 2.510 metros.
Fortaleza: 2.250 metros.
Izaña: 2.247 metros.
El Cabezón: 2.240 metros.

5. FIESTAS Y ESPECTACULOS
FETES ET SPECTACLES
FESTIVITIES AND SPECTACLES
FESTE UND SCHAUSPIELE

5.1. PLAYAS DE TENERIFE
PLAGES DE TENERIFE
THE BEACHES OF TENERIFE
STRÄNDE VON TENERIFFA

Santa Cruz de Tenerife

LAS TERESITAS. *LAS TERESITAS.*
LAS TERESITAS. *LAS TERESITAS.*

Situada en el barrio de San Andrés, a 9 kilómetres de la capital. Longitud: 1.450 metros. Características: arena negra y callaíllos. Acceso: pista que llega hasta la misma playa.

Située dans le quartir de San Andrés à 9 km de la capitale. Longueur: 1450 mètres. Caractéristiques: sable noir et gravier. Accès: piste qui arrive jusqu'à même la plage.

Situated in the San Andrés district, 9 km. from the capital. It is 1,450 metres long, and the sand is dark in colour. There is a road which leads to the beach itself.

Liegt im Stadtviertel von San Andrés, 9 km. von der Hauptstadt entfernt. Länge: 1.450 m. Kennzeichen: schwarzer Sand. Zugang: Strasse bis zum Strand vorhanden.

PLAYA DE ANTEQUERA.
PLAGE DE ANTEQUERA.
PLAYA DE ANTEQUERA.
PLAYA DE ANTEQUERA.

Situada a ocho millas de la capital. Longitud: 620 metros. Características: arena negra. Acceso: sólo por mar.

Située à 8 milles de la capitale. Longueur: 620 mètres. Caractéristiques: sable noir. Accès: seulement par mer.

It is 8 miles from the capital, and can only be reached from the sea. It is 620 metres long, and the sand dark coloured.

Liegt 8 Meilen von der Hauptstadt entfernt. Länge: 620 m. Kennzeichen: schwarzer Sand Zugang: Nur mit dem Schiff erreichbar.

La Laguna

LOS ARENALES. *LOS ARENALES.*
LOS ARENALES. *LOS ARENALES.*

Situada entre Bajamar y Punta de Hidalgo, a 24 km. de la capital. Longitud: 1.225 m. Características: arena negra y cantos rodados. Acceso: tiene acceso rodado.

Située entre Bajamar et Punta de Hidalgo. A 24 km de la capitale. Longueur: 1225 mètres. Caractéristiques: sable noir et galets. Accès: accès carrossable.

It lies between Bajamar and Punta de Hidalgo, 24 km. from the capital. Its length is 1,225 metres and there are boulders on the dark sand; it is easily accessible.

Liegt zwischen Bajamar und Punta de Hidalgo, 24 km von der Hauptstdat entfernt. Länge: 1,225 m. Kennzeichen: schwarzer Sand und Kiesefsteine. Zugang; mit dem Auto erreichbar.

La Orotava

EL BOYUYO Y ANCON.
EL BOYUYO ET ANCON.
EL BOYUYO AND ANCON.
EL BOYUYO UND ANCON.

Situada a 38 km. de la capital. Longitud: 87,50 y 183 metros. Características: arena negra. Acceso: tiene acceso rodado.

Située à 38 km de la capitale. Longueur: 87,50 mètres et 183 mètres. Caractéristiques: sable noir. Accès carrossable.

Situated at 38 km. from Santa Cruz, they have lengths of 87 and 183 metres. The sand is dark-coloured, and the beach can be easily reached.

Liegt 38 km. von der Hauptstadt entfernt. Länge:
87,5 und 183 m. Kennzeichen schwarzer Sand.
Zugang: mit dem Auto arreichbar.

Puerto de la Cruz

MARTIAÑEZ. *MARTIAÑEZ.*
MARTIAÑEZ. *MARTIAÑEZ.*

Situada a 38 km. de la capital. Longitud: 408 m.
Características: arena negra y callaíllos. Acceso: tiene acceso rodado hasta la misma playa. Instalaciones de luz y agua.

Située à 38 km de la capitale. Longueur: 408 mètres. Caractéristiques: sable noir et gravier. Accès: accès carrossable jusqu'à même la plage. Installations electriques et d'eau courante.

38 km. from the capital, it has a length of 408 metres, and dark sand. There are installations for water and light, and access is easy.

Liegt 38 km. von der Hauptstadt entfernt. Länge: 408 m. Kennzeichen: schwarzer Sand. Zugang: Man kann mit dem Auto bis an den Strand herenfahren. Lichtund Wasserinstallationen.

Los Realejos

PLAYA DEL CASTRO.
PLAGE DU CASTRO.
PLAYA DEL CASTRO.
PLAYA DEL CASTRO.

Situada a 47 km. de la capital. Longitud: 100 m. Características: arena negra. Accesos: pista hasta los acantilados y vereda a la playa.

Située à 47 km de la capitale. Longueur: 100 mètres. Caractéristiques: sable noir. Accès: piste jusqu'aux falaises et sentier a la plage.

47 km. from Santa Cruz, it has a length of 100 metres and the sand is dark; there is a road as far as the cliffs, and a path down to the beach.

Liegt 47 km. von der Hauptstadt entfernt. Länge: 100 m. Kennzeichen: schwarzer Sand Zugang: Fahrbahn bis zu den Klippen und Fussweg bis zum Strand vorhanden.

Icod de los Vinos

SAN MARCOS. *SAN MARCOS.*
SAN MARCOS. *SAN MARCOS.*

Situada a 63 km. de la capital. Longitud: 116 m. Características: arena negra. Acceso: la carretera llega hasta la misma playa. Tiene instalaciones de luz y agua.

Située à 63 km de la capitale. Longueur: 116 mètres. Caractéristiques: sable noir. Accès: la route arrive jusqu'à la plage. Installations électriques et eau courante.

It is 63 km. from the capital, has a length of 116 metres and sand that is dark in colour. The road takes you to the beach itself, and there are water and light installations.

Liegt 63 km. von der Hauptstadt entfernt. Länge: 116 m. Kennzeichen: schwarzer Sand. Zugang: Die Landstrasse geht bis an den Strand heran. Licht- und Wasserinstallationen vorhanden.

Garachico

EL PUERTITO. *EL PUERTITO.*
EL PUERTITO. *EL PUERTITO.*

Situada a 66 km. de la capital. Longitud: 60 m. Características: arena negra. Acceso: la carretera llega hasta la misma playa. Piscinas naturales en el punto llamado «El Caletón».

Située à 66 km de la capitale. Longueur: 60 mètres. Caractéristiques: sable noir. Accès: la route arrive jusqu'à la plage. Piscines naturelles au point appelé «El Caletón».

Situated at 66 km. from the capital; its length is 60 metres and the sand is dark; the road leads right top to the beach. At the point called «El Caletón» there are swimming pools.

Liegt 66 km von der Hauptstadt entfernt. Länge: 60 m. Kennzeichen: schawarzer Sand. Zugang: Die Landstrasse geht bis an den Strand heran. Salzwassser-Schwimmbecken am sogenannten Punkt «El Caletón».

Candelaria

LAS CALETILLAS. *LAS CALETILLAS.*
LAS CALETILLAS. *LAS CALETILLAS.*

Situada a 20 km. de la capital. Longitud: primera cala, 31 m.; segunda cala, 64 m.; tercera cala, 34 m. Acceso: pista asfaltada hasta la misma playa. Instalaciones de luz y agua.

Située à 20 km de la capitale. Longueur première crique, 31 mètres; deuxième crique: 64; troisième crique, 34 mètres. Accès: piste asphaltée jusqu'à la plage. Installations électriques et eau courante.

These are three coves 20 km. from Santa Cruz, the length of the firts is 31 metres, of the second 64 metres, and of the third 34 metres. There is a road that leads right up to the beaches, and there are installations for light and water.

Liegt 20 km. von der Hauptstadt entfernt. Länge: erste Bucht 31 m. zweite Bucht 64 m. dritte Bucht 34 m. Zugang Asphaltbahn bis zum Strand vorhanden. Licht- und Wasserinstallationen.

EL POZO. *EL POZO.*
EL POZO. *EL POZO.*

Longitud: 919 m. Características: arena negra, callaíllos y grandes cantos rodados. Acceso: la carretera llega hasta la misma playa.

Longueur: 919 mètres. Caractéristiques: sable noir, gravier et gros galets. Accès: la route arrive à la plage.

This has a length of 919 metres, the sand is dark, and there are pebbles and large rocks, it is easily accessible.

Länge: 919 m. Kennzeichen: schwarzer Sand und grosse Kieselsteine. Zugang: Die Landstrasse geht bis an den Strand heran.

PLAYA DE LA VIUDA.
PLAYA DE LA VIUDA.
PLAYA DE LA VIUDA.
PLAYA DE LA VIUDA.

Longitud: 750 metros. Características: arena negra y callaíllos. Acceso: pista que llega hasta el acantilado y vereda que baja a la playa.

Longueur: 750 mètres. Caractéristiques: sable noir et gravier. Accès: piste qui arrive aux falaises et sentier qui descend à la plage.

A beach 750 metres long with dark sand and pebbles. The road goes es far as the of the cliff, and there is a pach that runs down to the beach.

Länge: 750 m. Kennzeichen; schwarzer Sand. Zugang: Fahrbahn bis zu den Klippen und Fussweg bis zum Strand vorhanden.

Arafo

PLAYA DE LA LIMA.
PLAYA DE LA LIMA.
PLAYA DE LA LIMA.
PLAYA DE LA LIMA.

Longitud: 672 metros. Características: grandes cantos rodados. Acceso: pista que llega hasta la playa.

Longueur: 672 mètres. Caractéristiques: gros galets ronds. Accès: piste qui arrive à la plage.

On this beach, that is 672 metres long, there are many large rocks; the road leads to the beach.

Länge 672 m. Kennzeichen: grosse Kieselsteine. Zugang: Fahrbahn reich bis an den Strand.

Güimar

EL SOCORRO. *EL SOCORRO.*
EL SOCORRO. *EL SOCORRO.*

Situada a 34 km. de la capital. Longitud: 748 m. Características: grandes cantos rodados. Acceso: pista que llega hasta la playa.

Située à 34 km de la capitale. Longueur: 748 mètres. Caractéristiques: gros galets ronds. Accès: piste qui arrive à la plage.

34 km. from the capital, it has a length of 748 metres and there are rocks. There is a road to the beach.

Liegt 34 km. von der Hauptstadt entfernt. Länge: 748 m. Kennzeichen: grosse Kieselsteine. Zugang: Fhrbahn bis zum Strand.

EL PUERTITO. *EL PUERTITO.*
EL PUERTITO. *EL PUERTITO.*

Situada a 35 km. de la capital. Longitud: 1.600 m. Características: arena negra y callaíllos y cantos rodados. Acceso: la carretera llega hasta la misma playa. Instalaciones de luz y agua.

Située à 35 km de la capitale. Longueur: 1600 mètres. Caractéristiques: sable noir, gravier et galets ronds. Accès: la route arrive jusqu'à même la plage. Installations électriques et eau courante.

This beach is 1,600 metres long, and is 35 km. from the capital; the sand is dark, and there are pebbles and rocks. The road leads to the beach itself, and there are installations for light and water.

Liegt 35 km. von der Hauptstadt entfernt. Länge: 1.600 m. Kennzeichen; schwarzer Sand und Kieselsteine. Zugang: Fahrbahn bis an der Strand, Licht- und Wasserinstallationen vorhanden.

Fasnia

EL ROQUE. *EL ROQUE.*
EL ROQUE. *EL ROQUE.*

Situada a 53 km. de la capital. Longitud: 314 m. Características: arena negra y callaíllos. Acceso: pista que llega hasta el acantilado y vereda a la playa.

Située à 53 km de la capitale. Longeur: 314 mètres. Caractéristiques: sable noir et gravier. Accès: piste qui arrive aux falaises et sentier descendant à la plage.

53 km. from Santa Cruz, this beach of darkcoloured sand and pebbles is 314 metres long; there is a road to the cliff-top, and a path that runs down to the beach.

Liegt 53 km. von der Hauptstadt entfernt. Länge: 314 m. Kennzeichen: schwarzer Stand Zugang: Fahrbahn bis zu den Klippen und Fussweg bis zum Strand.

Arico

LOS ABRIGOS CHICOS.
LOS ABRIGOS CHICOS.
LOS ABRIGOS CHICOS.
LOS ABRIGOS CHICOS.

Situada a 70 kilómetros de la capital. Longitud: 150 metros. Características: arena negra y callaíllos. Acceso: pista hasta el Sanatorio y vereda a la playa.

Située à 70 km de la capitale. Longueur: 150 mètres. Caractéristiques: sable noir et gravier. Accès: piste jusqu'à l'hôpital et sentier à la plage.

70 km. from the capital, 150 metres long, it is a beach of dark sand and pebbes; a path leads down to the beach.

Liegt 70 km. von der Hauptstadt entfernt. Länge: 150 m. Kennzeichen: schwarzen Sand. Zuang: Fahrbahn bis zum Sanatorium und Fussweg bis zum Strand.

PLAYA DE ABONA. *PLAYA DE ABONA.*
PLAYA DE ABONA. *PLAYA DE ABONA.*

Situada a 69 kilómetros de la capital. Longitud: 74 m. Características: arena negra. Acceso: pista hasta el acantilado y vereda a la playa.

Située à 69 km de la capitale. Longueur: 74 mètres. Caractéristiques: sable noir. Accès: piste jusqu'aux falaises et sentier descendant à la plage.

74 metres long, 69 km. from the capital, and dark sand; there is a toad to the cliff-top, and a path that leads to the beach.

Liegt 69 km. von der Hauptstadt entfernt. Länge: 74 m. Kennzeichen: schwarzer Sand. Zugang: Fahrbahn bis zu den Klippen und Fussweg bis zum Strand.

Granadilla

EL MEDANO. *EL MEDANO.*
EL MEDANO. *EL MEDANO.*

Situada a 92 km. de la capital. Longitud: 1.750 m. Características: arena rubia. Acceso: la carretera llega hasta la playa. Instalaciones de luz y agua.

Située à 92 km de la capitale. Longueur: 1750 mètres. Caractéristiques: sable blond. Accès: la route arrive à la plage. Installations électriques et eau courante.

This beach is 92 km. from Santa Cruz, 1,750 metres long, and the sand is light in colour. The roads goes as far as the beach itself, and there are water and light installations.

Liegt 92 km. von der Hauptstadt entfernt. Länge: 1.750 m. Kennzeichen: goldener Sand. Zugang: Die Landstrasse führt bis an den Strand. Licht- und Wasserinstallationen vorhanden.

LA TEJITA. *LA TEJITA.*
LA TEJITA. *LA TEJITA.*

Situada a 93 km. de la capital. Longitud: 914 m. Características: arena rubia. Acceso: pista que llega hasta la playa.

Située à 93 km de la capitale. Longueur: 914 mètres. Caractéristiques: sable blond. Accès: piste qui arrive à la plage.

93 km. from the capital, 914 metres long, and light-coloured sand; the road leads to the beach.

Liegt 93 km. von der Hauptstadt entfernt. Länge: 914 m. Kennzeichen: goldener Sand. Zugang: Fahrbahn geht bis an den Strand heran.

San Miguel

Situada a 100 kilómetros de la capital. Longitud: 112 metros. Características: cantos rodados. Acceso: la pista llega hasta la playa.

Longueur: 112 mètres. Située à 100 km de la capitale. Caractéristiques: galets ronds. Accès: piste qui arrive à la plage.

This beach is 100 km. from Santa Cruz, and has a length of 112 metres; it is rocky. The road leads to the beach.

Liegt 100 km. von der Hauptstadt entfernt. Länge: 112 m. Kennzeichen: Kieselsteine. Zugang: Fahrbahn führt bis an den Strand.

Arona

LAS GALLETAS. *LAS GALLETAS.*
LAS GALLETAS. *LAS GALLETAS.*

Situada a 105 km. de la capital. Longitud: 650 metros. Características: arena negra y callaíllos. Acceso: la pista llega hasta la misma playa.

Située à 105 km de la capitale. Longueur: 650 mètres. Caractéristiques: sable et gravier. Accès: la piste arrive à la plage.

105 km. from the capital, 650 metres long, the sand is dark and there are pebbles. The road leadas to the beach.

Liegt 105 km. von der Hauptstadt entfernt. Länge: 650 m. Kennzeichen; schwarzer Sand. Zugang: Die Fahrbahn führt bis an den Strand heran.

LOS CRISTIANOS. *LOS CRISTIANOS.*
LOS CRISTIANOS. *LOS CRISTIANOS.*

Situada a 105 kilómetros de la capital. Longitud: 1.300 m. Características: arena rubia. Acceso: la carretera llega hasta la playa.

Située à 105 km de la capitale. Longueur: 1300 mètres. Caractéristiques: sable blond. Accès: la route arrive à la plage.

105 km. from the capital. 1,300 metres long, the sand is light-coloured. The road goes as far as the beach.

Liegt 105 km. von der Hauptstadt entfernt. Länge 1.300 m. Kennzeichen: goldener Sand. Zugang: Landstrasse führt bis an den Strand heran.

Adeje

PLAYA DE LA TROYA.
PLAYA DE LA TROYA.
PLAYA DE LA TROYA.
PLAYA DE LA TROYA.

Situada a 108 kilómetros de la capital. Longitud: 300 metros. Características: cantos rodados. Acceso: pista que llega hasta el acantilado y vereda hasta la playa.

Située à 108 km de la capitale. Longueur: 300 mètres. Caractéristiques: galets ronds. Accès: piste qui arrive aux falaises et sentier descendant à la plage.

108 km. from the capital, 300 metres long with rocks; there is a road to the cliff-top and a path down to the beach.

Liegt 108 km. von der Hauptstadt entfernt. Länge: 300 m. Kennzeichen: Kieselsteine. Zugang: Fahrbahn führt bis zu den Klippen und Fussweg bis zum Strand.

Santiago del Teide

LA ARENA. *LA ARENA.*
LA ARENA. *LA ARENA.*

Situada a 99 km. de la capital. Longitud: 147 m. Características: arena negra. Acceso: pista que llega hasta la misma playa.

Située à 99 km de la capitale. Longueur: 147 mètres. Caractéristiques: sable noir. Accès: piste qui arrive à la plage.

This beach is 99 km. from Santa Cruz, a length of 147 metres, and dark-coloured sand; the road goes as far as the beach.

Liegt 99 km. von der Hauptstadt entfernt. Länge: 147 m. Kennzeichen: schwarzer Sand. Zugang: Fahrbahn führt bis zum Strand.

PLAYA DE ARGEL. *PLAYA DE ARGEL.*
PLAYA DE ARGEL. *PLAYA DE ARGEL.*

Situada a 98 kilómetros de la capital. Longitud: 550 m. Características: arena negra en verano, cantos rodados en invierno. Acceso: pista hasta el acantilado y vereda a la playa.

Située à 98 km de la capitale. Longueur: 550 mètres. Caractéristiques: sable noir en été, galets ronds en hiver. Accès: piste jusqu'à la falaise et sentier à la plage.

98 km. from the capital and 550 metres long; there is dark sand in summer, and rocks in winter. There is a road to the top of the cliffs, and a path down to the beach.

Liegt 98 km. von der Hauptstadt entfernt. Länge: 550 m. Kennzeichen: schwarzer Sand im Sommer, Kieselsteine im Winter, Zugang: Fahrbahn führt bis zu den Klippen und Fussweg bis zum Strand.

PLAYA PUERTO SANTIAGO.
PLAYA PUERTO SANTIAGO.
PLAYA PUERTO SANTIAGO.
PLAYA PUERTO SANTIAGO.

Situada a 97 kilómetros de la capital. Longitud: 63 metros. Características: arena negra. Acceso: pista hasta el pueblo y vereda a la playa.

Située à 97 km de la capitale. Longueur: 63 mètres. Caractéristiques: sable noir. Accès: piste jusqu'au village et sentier à la plage.

97 km. from Santa Cruz, a length of 63 metres, and dark sand; the road goes as far as the village, and then there is a path to the beach.

Liegt 97 km. von der Hauptstadt entfernt. Länge: 63 m. Kennzeichen: schwarzer Sand. Zugang: Fahrbahn bis zum Dorf und Fussweg bis zum Strand.

5.2. DEPORTES-SPORTS
SPORTS-SPORT

La práctica de todos los deportes tiene en estas islas escenario adecuado. La pesca submarina, la natación y cuantos deportes acuáticos existen, tienen en playas y piscinas gran cantidad de aficionados. Campos de tenis, pelota vasca, tiro de pichón y magníficos campos de golf en terreno ondulado y césped perfecto ofrecen al viajero sus mil posibilidades de entretenimiento.

También tendrá ocasión de contemplar los deportes tradicionales, tales como las riñas de gallos, el juego del palo, palo, especie de esgrima sostenida con dos varas largas, y la famosa lucha canaria, de remoto origen, que requiere gran habilidad y fuerza y constituye un espectáculo del mayor interés en el que no están permitidos los golpes.

Asimismo es tradicional el «salto del regatón» o de la garrocha, que se practica especialmente en la isla de San Miguel de La Palma.

Ces îles sont le lieu adéquat pour la pratique de tous les sports. La pêche sous-marine, la nata-

tion et tous les sports sur l'eau. Il y a des piscines et des plages avec quantité d'amateurs. Des terrains de tennis, pelote basque, tir au pigeon et de magnifiques terrains de golf sur surface ondulée et gazon en parfait état, offrent au voyageur mille possibilités pour ses loisirs.

Il pourra également contempler des sports traditionnels, comme les disputes de coqs, le jeu du «palo» (bâton), espèce d'escrime réalisée avec deux longs bâtons, et la fameuse lutte des Canaries, d'origine fort ancienne, qui exige gande habileté et force, et constitue un spectacle du plus grand intérêt; les coups ne sont pas permis.

Il es traditionnel, également, le «salto del regatón» ou de la perche, qui est particulièrement pratiquée sur l'île de San Miguel de La Palma.

These islands are the ideal background for all kinds of sports. Underwater spearfishing, water ski-ing and other water sports have a tremendous following among the visitors to our beaches, while tennis and pelota courts, clay pigeon ranges and magnificent golf courses, with their softly rolling links and perfect greens, offer an unlimited variety of entertainment for the visitor.

Tourists may also enjoy the spectacle of more traditional sports such as cock-fighting, the game of palo palo, a kind of fencing with long staves, and the famous Canary Island wrestling matches whose origins are lost in time. This sport requires great skill and strength and matches are of particular interest since the rules forbid the striking of blows.

Also traditional is the «salto del regatón» (pole-vaulting over the horns of a bull) which is particularly popular on the island of San Miguel de La Palma.

Auf diesen Inseln ist Gelegenheit zur Ausübung aller Sport-arten. Das Unterseefischen, Schwimmen und alle möglichen Wassersportarten haben am Strand und in Swimming-Pools einen Haufen Anhänger. Tennisplätze, Basketnball, Hahnenschiessen und grossartige Golfplätze auf welligem Grund und perfektem Rasen bieten dem Reisenden tausend Möglichkeiten zur Unterhaltung. Ebenfalls hat er Gelegenheit, die traditionellen Sportarten zu betrachten, wie Hahnenkämpfe, das Stockspiel, wo der Stock eine Art Degen ist, gehalten von zwei langen Stangen, und der berühmte kanarische Kampf, dessen Ursprung weit zurückliegt und welcher grosse Geschicklichkeit und Kraft erfordert und ein Schauspiel grössten Interesses darstellt, bei dem keine Schläge erlaubt sind.

Ebenso ist der «Stabsprung» traditionell, der vor allem auf der Insel San Miguel de La Palma praktiziert wird.

5.3. ESPECTACULOS-SPECTACLES SHOWS-SCHAUSPIELE

Fiestas-Fêtes
Feasts-Feste

Del 1 al 10 de mayo, las conmemorativas de la Cruz y de la fundación de Santa Cruz de Tenerife, las del aniversario de la derrota de Sir Horacio Nelson, en la capital (25 de julio), las de San Benito Abad en La Laguna, primer domingo del mes de julio (del más rancio sabor folklórico), Octava del Corpus, y Romería de San Isidro en La Orotava; las del Gran Poder de Dios y de la Virgen del Carmen, en el Puerto de la Cruz (2.ª quincena de julio), la del Santísimo Cristo de La Laguna (14 de septiembre), la de la Virgen de Candelaria, en la que se realiza el simulacro pastoril de la aparición de la Virgen a los Guanches (14 de agosto).

Du 1 su 10 mai, les fêtes commémoratives de la Croix et de la Fondation de Santa Cruz de Tenerife, celles de l'anniversaire de la défaite de Sir Horace Nelson dans la capitale (25 juillet), celles de St. Benito Abbé à La Laguna, premier dimanche de juillet (de la plus ancienne saveur folklorique), Octave de la Fête-Dieu et Pélerinage de San Isidro à La Orotava; celles du «Gran Poder et de la Vierge du Carmen au Puerto de la Cruz (2ème quinzaine de juillet) celles du Santo Cristo de La Laguna (14 septembre), celle de la Vierge de la Candelaria où l'on réalise le simulacre de l'apparition de la Vierge aux Guanches (14 août).

The foundation of Santa Cruz de Tenerife is celebrated from May lst to 10th, the defeat of Admiral Nelson on, July 25th (in Santa Cruz), San Benito Abad in La Laguna on the first Sunday of July (one of the festivals in which island folklore can best be seen), the Octave of Corpus Christi and Romeria of San Isidro in La Orotava. There are celebrations in honour of the «Virgen del Carmen» in Puerto de la Cruz during the second fortnight in Juli, in honour of the Christ of La Laguna on september 14th, and that in honour of the Virgin of Candelaria on August 14th when there is a reenactment of the finding of the Virgin by the Guanches (the primitive inhabitants of the Canary Islands).

Vom 1.-10. Mai Gedächtnisfaiern des Kreuzes und der Stadtgründung Santa Cruz de Tenerife. Am 25. Juli Gedächtnisfeier der Niederlage des englischen Admirals Nelson. Erster Sonntag im Juli Fest des heiligen Benedikt in La Laguna, Oktav von Fronlsichnam und am folgenden Sonntag San Isidro-Wallfahrt in La Orotava. Fest Gran Poder de Dios und zu Ehren der Virgen del Carmen in Puerto de la

Cruz (zweite Juli-Hälfte). Volksfest zu Ehren des Santísimo Cristo de La Laguna (14. September). Fest der Virgen de Candelaria, bei dem in einem Hirtenspiel die Erscheinung der Jungfrau Maria von den guanches dargestellt wird (14 August).

Folklore musical
Folklore musical
Typical dances of the island
Folklore

LA ISA. *LA ISA.*
LA ISA. *LA ISA.*

Canto y baile de parranda, de alegre romería —la jota atlántica—, que tiene hermandad legítima con cantos y bailes americanos —el pericón argentino, corridos mejicanos, danzas chilenas...—.

Chant et danse de joyeux pèlerinage. La «jota» de l'Atlantique, qui a une fraternité légitime avec les chants et danses américains. Le pericon argentin, les corridos mexicains, les danses chiliennes.

A merry song and dance like an Atlantic Jota, has things in common with some South American songs and dances, such as the Argentine Pericón the Mexican Corridos and dances from Chile, etc.

Gesang und Tanz bei vergnügten Festen, fröhlichen Wallfahrten —genannt atlantische Jota (Volkstanz und -lied aus Aragonien und Valencia)—, der mit süd-amerikanischen Gesängen und Tänzen verwandt ist, wie z.B. mit dem argentinischen pericón, den mexikanischen corridos, chilenischen Tänzen...

FOLIA. *FOLIA.*
FOLIA. *FOLIA.*

Señorial bolero de pasos lentos y reposados. Canto donde métrica y melodía quedan supeditadas a la libre expresión anímica del que canta, y muchas veces al sentido de la copla, alargando y acortando frases. Ritmo cadente, propio de las coplas tristes y trágicas de Andalucía, recordando al mismo tiempo a los boleros mallorquines.

Boléro seigneurial à pas lents et tranquilles. Chant dont la métrique et la mélodie sont liés à la libre expression de celui qui chante et souvent du sens de la chanson, allongeant et raccourcissant les phrases. Rythme cadencé, propre aux couplets tristes et tragiques d'Andalousie, rappelant à la fois les boléros majorquins.

A seigniorial bolero with slow steps; the music and words can be adapted by the singer in order to give greater expression; the rhythm recalls the tragic songs of Andalucía and also the boleros of Mallorca.

Herrschaftlicher Bolero mit langsamen und ruhigen Schritten. Gesang, bei dem Metrik und Melodie frei der Ausdrucksweise des Sängers überlassen werden, der je nach Inhalt des Liedes die Sätze kürzen oder verlängern kann. Es ist ein betonter Rhythmus, wie er bei den traurigen und tragischen Volksliedern Andalusiens zu finden ist. Gleichzeitig erinnert er an die Boleros aus Mallorca.

LA SEGUIDILLA. *LA SEGUIDILLA.*
LA SEGUIDILLA. *LA SEGUIDILLA.*

Con sus aires manchegos y sus coplas andaluzas, en alegre rueda de danzas.

Avec ses airs de La Manche et ses couplets andalous dans une allègre ronde de danses.

With couplets from Andalucía and airs from La Mancha, is a gay dance.

Wird im Kreis getanzt. Ihre Melodien kommen aus der Mancha und ihre Verse aus Andalusien.

LAS SALTONAS. *LAS SALTONAS.*
LAS SALTONAS. *LAS SALTONAS.*

Jota en rueda, un poco fandango.

Jota en ronde, un peu fandango.

Danced in a ring is rather like a fandango.

Jota (Lied und Tanz aus Aragonien und Valencia), bei der sich die Tänzer im Kreis aufstellen. Sie ähnelt ein wenig den fandangos aus dem Süden Spaniens.

LA MALAGUEÑA CANARIA.
LA MALAGUEÑA CANARIA.
THE CANARIAN MALAGUEÑA.
DIE KANARISCHE MALAGUEÑA.

Algo de Málaga y algo de Huelva, con una coreografía de verdadero minueto. Alegórico triunfo de la virilidad y la fuerza frente a lo femenino, en el baile de un solo hombre con todas las bailaoras. Canto lento donde la tragedia se canta y se baila a la manera del Sur peninsular. Canciones de muerte para sentirlas bailando.

Quelque chose de Málaga et quelque chose de Huelva, avec une chorégraphie de véritable menuet. Triomphe allégorique de la virilité et de la force face au féminin dans le bal d'un seul homme avec toutes les danseuses. Chant lent où la tragédie se chante et se danse à la manière du sud de la péninsule. Chansons de la mort pour les sentir en dansant.

With something from Málaga and something from Huelva, has the steps of a real minuet; danced by one boy and several girls, it is an allegorical triumph of male virility and power. The song is slow and tragic, performed similarly to those of southern Spain.

Besitzt Eigentümlichkeiten aus Malaga und aus Huelva und wird von den Bewohnern mit der Anmut des Menuetts getanzt. Der Tanz, bei dem nur ein Mann mit mehreren Tänzarinnen auftritt, ist eine Allegorie des Triumphs der Virilität und der Kraft gegenüber der Weiblichkeit. Es sind gezogene und langsame Melodien, die man wie in Südspanien singt und tanzt. Wenn wir den Tänzern zusehen, spüran wir, wie sie diese vom Tode spachenden Lieder leben.

EL SANTO DOMINGO.
EL SANTO DOMINGO.
EL SANTO DOMINGO.
EL SANTO DOMINGO.

Danza netamente religiosa, que se baila ante la imagen sagrada, con astas de madera, cintas de colores que se cruzan, medios aros floridos, en parejas sueltas o en filas. Música de flauta de caña y tamboril rústico, con guitarras e instrumentos de cuerdas. Melodía de antigua canción andaluza del siglo XV.

Danse nettement religieuse qui se danse devant la sainte image avec des hampes de bois, des rubans de couleurs qui se croisent, demi-cerceaux fleuris, en couples séparés ou en file. Musique de flûte de jonc et tambourin rustique, avec guitares et instruments cordes. Mélodie d'ancienne chanson andalouse du à 15° siècle.

Is a religious dance which is performed before a holy image with wooden sticks, crossing coloured ribbons and flowered half hoops, by single couples or dancers in line. The melody is from an ancient Andalusian song of the 15th century, the accompaniment being provided by a wooden flute and rustic drum with guitars and other string instruments.

Ist ein rein religiöser Tanz, der vor dem Heiligenbild ausgeführt wird. Die Tänzer halten Stangen, farbige sich kreuzende Bänder oder Blumenreifen in den Händen, wobei sie sich zu einzelnen Paaren oder ganzen Reihen gruppieren. Flöten, einfache Tamburine, Gitarren und Streichinstrumente stellen die Begleitung zu diesem Tanz dar. Die Melodie stammt aus einem alten andalusischen Volkstanz aus dem XV. Jahrhundert.

EL TAJARASTE. *EL TAJARASTE.*
EL TAJARASTE. *EL TAJARASTE.*

La danza «el canario» que bailara el Rey Sol en la Corte de Francia, con indumentaria de plumas y pieles, memoria del primitivo guanche de Tenerife. Estas danzas o aires rítmicos fueron populares en el mundo entero. Para el «tajaraste» de la isla de La Gomera, acompañada de tambor, se cantan viejos romances y endechas, que se remontan, muchos a la época de la conquista de las islas, relatando milagros e historias de amores desgraciados. Además: EL TANGO HERREÑO y EL «TANGUILLO» —fandanguillo de Tenerife—.

La Danse «el canario» que dansait le Roi Soleil à la Cour de France avec un costume de plumes et de peaux, en mémoire du premier guanche de Ténérife. Ces danses et airs rythmiques furent populaires dans le monde entier. Pour la «tajaraste» de l'île de La Gomera, avec accompagnement de tambours, on chante de vielles romances qui remontent, pour la plupart, à l'époque de la conquête des îles et relatent les miracles et de malheureuses histoires d'amour. En outre: LE TANGO HERREÑO et LE TANGUILLO. Fandanguillo de Ténérife.

The dance known as «El Canario» which was danced by the Sun King at the French Cour in a costume of skins and feathers, recalling the primitive Guanches of Teherife. These dances became popular all over the world. The Tajaraste of Gomera Island is accompanied by a drum, and many of the songs date from the time of the conquest of the islands, telling of Miracles and unhappy love affairs. There is also the TANGO HERREÑO and the «TANGUILLO», the fandango of Tenerife.

Its der sogenannte Tanz «el canario», den der Sonnenkönig am Königshof von Frankreich, angetan mit Federn und Fellen, aus denen einst die Kleidung der guanches von Teneriffa bestand, vortrug. Diese Tänze oder Rhythmen waren in der granzen Welt bekannt. Auf der Insel Gomera wird der tajaraste von Trommeln begleitet. Dazu werden Romanzen und Trauerweisen gesungen, die zum grossen Teil auf die Eroberungsepoche der Inseln zurückgehen und von Wundern und unglücklichen Liebesgeschichten erzählen.

Ausserdem gibt es den TANGO von der Insel Hierro und dem «TANGUILLO» von Teneriffa, der dem fandanguillo aus Andalusien ähnelt.

6. TURISMO

6.1. EXCURSIONES DESDE SANTA CRUZ DE TENERIFE
EXCURSIONS PARTANT DE SANTA CRUZ DE TENERIFE
EXCURSIONS FROM SANTA CRUZ DE TENERIFE
EXKURSIONEN AB SANTA CRUZ DE TENERIFE

a) La Laguna, Monte de Las Mercedes (Pico del Inglés), Tejina, Bajamar (Playa), Tacoronte (Golf Club) y regreso, 74 km.

b) La Laguna, Tacoronte, Orotava, Puerto de la Cruz (jardín botánico), San Juan de la Rambla, Icod (Drago Milenario) y el Tanque (vista de Garachico), 144 km.
c) La Esperanza (bosque), Izaña (Observatorio), Montaña Blanca (Ascensión al Pico del Teide), Los Roques, Azulejos, Llano de Ucanca (Parador Nacional), Portillo de la Villa, Valle de La Orotava y regreso por la Carretera General del Norte, 150 km.
d) La Esperanza, Izaña, Montaña Blanca, Azulejos, Llano de Ucanca, Boca de Tauce, Vilaflor, Granadilla, El Médano (Playa), Güimar y regreso, 181 km.
e) Candelaria (Basílica), Güimar y regreso, 68 km.
f) La Laguna, Monte de Las Mercedes, Taborno, Vista de Taganana, San Andrés, Santa Cruz, 47 km.
g) Viaje de Circunvalación de la isla, 252 km.

a) *La Laguna, Monte de las Mercedes (Pico del Inglés), Tejina, Bajamar (Plage), Tacoronte (Golf Club) et retour, 74 km.*
b) *La Laguna, Tacoronte, Orotava, Puerto de la Cruz (jardin botanique), San Juan de la Rambla, Icod (Dragonnier millénaire) et El Tanque (vue de Garachico), 144 km.*
c) *La Esperanza (bois), Izaña (Observatoire), Montaña Blanca (Ascension au Pic du Teide), Los Roques, Azulejos, Llano de Ucanca (Parador National), Portillo de la Villa, Valle de La Orotava et retour par la Route Générale du Nord, 150 km.*
d) *La Esperanza, Izaña, Montaña Blanca, Azulejos, Llano de Ucanca, Boca de Tauce, Vilaflor, Granadilla, El Médano (plage), Güimar et retour, 181 km.*
e) *Candelaria (Basilique), Güimar et retour, 68 km.*
f) *La Laguna, Monte de las Mercedes, Taborno, Vista de Taganana, San Andrés, Santa Cruz, 47 km.*
g) *Voyage autour de l'île, 252 km.*

a) La Laguna, Monte de las Mercedes (Pico del Inglés), Tejina, Bajamar (Beach), Tacoronte (Golf Club) and back, 74 km.
b) La Laguna, Tacoronte, Orotava, Puerto de la Cruz (Botanical Gardens), San Juan de la Rambla, Icod (thousandyear old Dragontree) and El Tanque (with a visit to Garachico), 144 km.
c) La Esperanza (Forest), Izaña (the Observatory), Montaña Blanca (with the possibility of climbing Mount Teide), Los Roques, Azulejos, Llano de Ucanca (Parador National-State-run Hotel), Portillo de la Villa, Valle de La Orotava, and back by the main North road. 150 km.
d) La Esperanza, Izaña, Montaña Blanca, Azulejos, Llano de Ucanca, Boca de Tauce, Vilaflor, Granadilla, El Médano (Beach), Güimar, and back to Santa Cruz, 181 km.
e) Candelaria (the Basilica), Güimar and back, 68 km.
f) La Laguna, Monte de las Mercedes, Taborno, Vista de Taganana, San Andrés, and back to Santa Cruz, 47 km.
g) A trip right round the island, 252 km.

a) *La Laguna, Monte (Berg) de Las Mercedes (Pico del Inglés), Tejina, Bajamar (Strand), Tacoronte (Golf-platz) und Rückkehr, 74 km.*
b) *La Laguna, Tacoronte, Orotava, Puerto de la Cruz (botanischer Garten), San Juan de la Rambla, Icod (tausendjähriger Drachenbaum) und El Tanque (Blick auf Garachico), 144 km.*
c) *La Esperanza (Wald), Izaña (Observatorium), Montaña Blanca (Aufstieg zum Berggipfel des Teide), Los Roques, Azulejos, Llano de Ucanca (Parador), Portillo de la Villa, Valle (Tal) de La Orotava und Rückfahrt über die nördiche Hauptlandstrasse. 150 km.*
d) *La Esperanza, Izaña, Montaña Blanca (weisser Berg), Azulejos, Llano de Ucanca, Boca de Tauce, Vilaflor, Granadilla, El Médano (Strand), Güimar und Rückfahrt, 181 km.*
e) *Candelaria (Basilika), Güimar und Rückfahrt, 68 km.*
f) *La Laguna, Monte (Berg) de Las Mercedes, Taborno, Vista de Taganana, San Andrés, Santa Cruz, 47 km.*
g) *Rundfahrt um die Insel, 252 km.*

6.2. DISTANCIAS DE LA CAPITAL A: DISTANCES ENTRE LA CAPITALE ET: DISTANCES FROM SANTA CRUZ DE TENERIFE: ENTFERNUNGEN VON DER HAUPTSTADT NACH:

	km.
La Laguna	10
Las Mercedes	19
Tacoronte	20
La Orotava	36
Puerto de la Cruz	39
Icod	61
La Esperanza	16
Über den Berg La Esperanza	53
El Portillo über La Orotava	64
Candelaria	23
Güimar	31
Granadilla	82
El Médano	93
Los Cristianos	105
Vilaflor	89
Puerto Santiago (Acantilados de los Gigantes)	92

INDICE

Págs.

Entre Africa y Europa 4
Tenerife, continente en miniatura 14
Santa Cruz 24
La Laguna, camino del Norte 34
El Valle de La Orotava 44
El Jardín Botánico 61
La isla baja 64
Lo que no conviene dejarse atrás 78
Las Cañadas y el Pico del Teide 88
El amplio Sur 96
De Santa Cruz a Los Cristianos 106
Los confines de la isla 114
La Palma, La Gomera y El Hierro 121
Usos, Folklore y Gastronomía 134
Comunicaciones interiores e interinsulares 150

PUBLICACIONES EVEREST SOBRE LAS ISLAS CANARIAS

- **GUÍAS ARTÍSTICO-TURÍSTICAS**

— GRAN CANARIA-LANZAROTE-FUERTEVENTURA, por M. González Sosa.
Ediciones en español, francés, inglés y alemán.

— TENERIFE-LA PALMA-GOMERA-HIERRO, por Enrique García Ramos.
Ediciones en español, francés, inglés y alemán.

— COSTAS DE ESPAÑA, por J. A. García Barquero.
Edición en español.

— Guía Informativa de Gran Canaria, Lanzarote y Fuerteventura (español, francés, inglés, alemán y sueco).

- **COLECCIÓN IBÉRICA**

— FUERTEVENTURA EN COLOR (español, francés, inglés y aleman).

— GOMERA-HIERRO EN COLOR (español, francés, inglés y alemán).

— GRAN CANARIA EN COLOR (español, francés, inglés y alemán).

— LANZAROTE EN COLOR (español, francés, inglés y alemán).

— LA PALMA EN COLOR (español, francés, inglés y alemán).

— TENERIFE EN COLOR (español, francés, inglés y alemán).

- **COLECCIÓN HISPÁNICA**
- — FUERTEVENTURA, por Carlos J. Taranilla
  (Ediciones en español, francés, inglés y alemán).
- — GOMERA-HIERRO, por Carlos J. Taranilla
  (Ediciones en español, francés, inglés y alemán).
- — LA PALMA, por Carlos J. Taranilla
  (Ediciones en español, francés, inglés y alemán).
- — TENERIFE por Domingo Manfredi Cano
  (Ediciones en español, francés, inglés y alemán).

- **CLUB EVEREST**
- — ESPAÑA TURÍSTICA

- **MAPAS TURÍSTICOS DE ESPAÑA**
- — MAPA CARTOGRÁFICO DE LAS ISLAS CANARIAS.
- — MAPA TURÍSTICO DE LANZAROTE Y PLANO DE ARRECIFE.
- — GUÍA-CALLEJERO DE LAS PALMAS DE GRAN CANARIA.
- — PLANO-CALLEJERO DE LAS PALMAS DE GRAN CANARIA.